WILLIAMS-SONOMA

Cooking from the Farmers' Market

GENERAL EDITOR
Chuck Williams

RECIPES
Georgeanne Brennan

PHOTOGRAPHY
Richard Eskite

TIME
LIFE
BOOKS

TIME-LIFE BOOKS
Time-Life Books is a division of Time Life Inc.
Time-Life is a trademark of Time Warner Inc. U.S.A.

TIME-LIFE CUSTOM PUBLISHING
Vice President and Publisher: Terry Newell
Vice President of Sales and Marketing: Neil Levin
Director of Financial Operations: J. Brian Birky
Director of Acquisitions: Jennifer L. Pearce

WILLIAMS-SONOMA
Founder and Vice-Chairman: Chuck Williams
Book Buyer: Victoria Kalish

WELDON OWEN INC.
President: John Owen
Vice President and Publisher: Wendely Harvey
Chief Operating Officer: Larry Partington
Vice President International Sales: Stuart Laurence
Associate Publisher: Lisa Atwood
Managing Editor: Val Cipollone
Consulting Editor: Norman Kolpas
Copy Editor: Sharon Silva
Series Design: Kari Perin, Perin+Perin
Book Design: Diane Dempsey
Production Director: Stephanie Sherman
Production Manager: Jen Dalton
Production Editor: Sarah Lemas
Food Stylist: Pouké
Prop Stylist: Laura Ferguson
Photo Production Coordinator: Juliann Harvey
Photo Assistant: Kevin Hossler
Food Styling Assistants: Jeff Tucker, Michelle Syracuse
Glossary Illustrations: Alice Harth

A NOTE ON WEIGHTS AND MEASURES
All recipes include customary U.S. and metric measurements. Metric conversions are based on a standard developed for these books and have been rounded off. Actual weights may vary.

The Williams-Sonoma Lifestyles Series
conceived and produced by Weldon Owen Inc.
814 Montgomery Street, San Francisco, CA 94133

In collaboration with Williams-Sonoma
3250 Van Ness Avenue, San Francisco, CA 94109

Separations by Colourscan Overseas Co. Pte. Ltd.
Printed in Singapore by Tien Wah Press (Pte.) Ltd.

A WELDON OWEN PRODUCTION
Copyright © 1999 Weldon Owen Inc.
All rights reserved, including the right of
reproduction in whole or in part in any form.

First printed in 1999
10 9 8 7 6 5 4 3 2 1

Library of Congress
Cataloging-in-Publication Data

Brennan, Georgeanne
    Cooking from the farmers' market / general editor,
Chuck Williams; recipes by Georgeanne Brennan;
photography by Richard Eskite.
        p.   cm. — (Williams-Sonoma lifestyles)
    Includes index.
    ISBN 0-7370-2013-x
    1. Cookery, American. 2. Farm Produce—
United States I. Williams, Chuck. II. Title.
III. Series.
TX715.B38344 1999
    641.5973— dc21   98-35969
                                      CIP

A NOTE ON NUTRITIONAL ANALYSIS
Each recipe is analyzed for significant nutrients per serving. Not included in the analysis are ingredients that are optional or added to taste, or are suggested as an alternative or substitution either in the recipe or in the recipe introduction or accompanying tip. In recipes that yield a range of servings, the analysis is for the middle of that range.

Contents

Welcome

When I was a boy growing up in northern Florida, we didn't buy vegetables and fruits in supermarkets. Our produce came from small shops or horse-drawn wagons that brought the harvest of local farms to us.

Today, with the proliferation of farmers' markets, we are once again shopping close to the source. Communities everywhere have farmers' markets filled with locally grown bounty. Their presence reflects a growing interest in good food and cooking and an awareness of the benefits in taste and nutrition that come from enjoying the freshest fruits and vegetables from local farms.

This book celebrates farmers' markets with a bumper crop of inspired recipes. It also includes information on buying high-quality seasonal produce and putting it to its best use.

Here are a few tips I've gathered during a lifetime of frequenting farmers' markets: First, be flexible. You might not find what you were planning to buy, but see instead an unexpected ingredient that captures your imagination. Don't pass it up. Although it's tempting to fill your basket, buy only what you need. Finally, talk with the growers. Let them guide you to the best of the season. A visit to the farmers' market can be a deliciously enlightening experience.

Chuck Williams

Spring

Strawberries (above) are perhaps the finest and simplest of springtime pleasures. They come in many shapes and sizes, all waiting to delight. You can sometimes find *fraises des bois*, small, intensely flavorful wild berries that are some of the season's best. Scallops (opposite page), a bellwether of spring, are sautéed just until lightly browned for a salad that can be served as a starter or light main course.

Enjoying the Pleasures of Spring

In springtime, all manner of vegetables and the year's early fruits await the eager cook. Bring along a big basket when you visit the farmers' market this time of year—the jewels of the season are hard to resist.

Leafy greens abound, including all kinds of tender young lettuces; bunches of young, dark green spinach; spear-shaped heads of crisp, mildly bitter Belgian endive; and refreshing, peppery watercress. In all cases, look for those specimens with bright colors and fresh-looking leaves, with no signs of wilting.

Fava (broad) beans, English peas, and sugar snap peas are some of the finest foods the season has to offer. Be sure to seek out fresh, plump pods in all cases. And don't hesitate to ask a market vendor for a taste of a sugar snap pea, which should be snappy in texture and pleasantly sweet.

Stalks of asparagus are another seasonal favorite, so tender that they need only a little preparation (opposite, left) and quick cooking. The spring crop of artichokes, often small in size, yields specimens that require just a quick trimming (opposite, right) before they are ready to cook.

Some of the season's most delicate treats are underground roots, tubers, and bulbs that are harvested in their immature forms. Look for new potatoes, for instance, prized for their sweet flesh and tissue-thin skins. You may also find baby beets, carrots, turnips, and other root vegetables; baby leeks and green garlic from the onion family; and tiny summer squashes.

Among the fresh fruits available in spring, strawberries are a special treat, plump and sweet.

They are indeed the pride of the spring market. Blueberries, too, will begin to appear as summer nears. And, depending on location, farmers at your local market may proffer tropical fruits this time of year. Bananas are best early in the season, papayas fine throughout, and mangoes at their finest in the month or two before summer. Early apricots and cherries are another springtime treat, forerunners of the stone fruit harvest of summer.

In addition, some farmers' markets carry seasonal foods well suited to the center of the plate. Seek out lamb, at its youngest and most tender this time of year. And seafood purveyors may offer such delicacies as Dungeness and soft-shell crabs, scallops, or fresh salmon pulled from ocean waters.

Cooking with Ease

Springtime's sweet, tender specialties are well suited to quick, simple cooking methods that maintain their delicate flavor and texture. Sautéing—quickly cooking ingredients in a pan over high heat with just a little bit of oil or butter—seals in an

TECHNIQUES

TRIMMING ASPARAGUS

In springtime, spears of asparagus push up toward the sun, developing their signature fresh flavor and tender-crisp texture. Almost all of the spear is edible. To trim, simply bend near the cut end and the tough part will naturally break away.

TRIMMING ARTICHOKES

To trim a young artichoke, cut off the stem. Pull off all the tough outer leaves. Cut off the top one-third. Pare off the dark outer skin. Put trimmed artichokes in water to which lemon juice has been added to prevent discoloration.

ingredient's flavorful juices and takes just moments to do. Spring Lettuces with Grapefruit and Sautéed Scallops (page 47) and Pan-Seared Halibut with Sautéed Baby Vegetables (page 62) are both good examples of this principle. Stir-frying, the technique of rapidly cooking ingredients cut into small pieces by tossing them in a large pan over high heat, is another way to prepare foods that require a minimum of cooking.

Summer

Melons (below, right) enjoy the spotlight at farmers' markets in summer. Look for (from bottom left) Galia, Canary, cantaloupe, and yellow and pink watermelons. But the market offers more than fruits and vegetables. Flowers (above) are often part of the mix.

Delighting in Summer

The bright promise of spring reaches generous fulfillment in summer, as farmers' markets overflow with wonderful fresh foods. Wherever you turn, stalls are piled high with sun-ripened fruits and colorful vegetables.

Summer fruits are, hands down, the year's juiciest. This is prime time for melons, from the familiar cantaloupe, honeydew, and watermelon to the more exotic Crenshaw, casaba, and Charentais. All show ripeness by being heavy for their size; sniff small ones near their stem ends for signs of sweetness, too.

Heaviness also indicates good summer stone fruits such as peaches, nectarines, and plums, along with the apricots and cherries that first appeared in spring. Ripe specimens yield to gentle pressure. Apricots, peaches, and nectarines also give off a sweet scent. Look, too, for the early crop of richly perfumed figs.

Berries are at their best this time of year. Early season strawberries and blueberries give way to blackberries, raspberries, and boysenberries. While you should look for well-formed, plump, deeply colored fruits, the best way to test is to taste.

In this season of abundant fruit, it isn't surprising that the finest vegetables available are those that are botanically members of the fruit family: tomatoes, bell peppers (capsicums), eggplants (aubergines), cucumbers, summer squashes, and avocados.

Look, as well, to farmers' markets this time of year for the best fresh corn, which will have the sweetest flavor when cooked as soon as possible after picking. Individual ears should have bright green husks, fresh-looking silk, and smooth, plump kernels. Fresh shelling beans, such as cranberry beans, are also at their peak of flavor now.

New crops of onions and garlic are harvested in summer. Seek out such onion varieties as the elongated red torpedo and the small, flattened Italian cipolline. And a wide range of potatoes may be found, including such buttery-tasting yellow-fleshed varieties as Yukon gold and Yellow Finn. Look for long, slender, waxy fingerling potatoes, too.

The hot sun of summer pushes a wide variety of fresh herbs into their fragrant glory. While most are now available fresh year-round, you're likely to see outstanding displays of basil, chervil, chives, cilantro, dill, marjoram, mint, oregano, parsley, rosemary, sage, tarragon, and thyme in the summer months.

Cooking Quickly

Like spring, summer cooking reflects the spirit of the ingredients found at market this time of year—many of which are perfectly ripe and tender and ready to eat au naturel. Indeed, some dishes, salads for instance, require no cooking at all. On those occasions when cooking is called for, grilling is far and away the method of choice. The intense heat of the grill cooks food quickly, be it fruit, vegetable, fish, fowl, or meat, adding a lick of smoky flavor in the process. You'll find recipes that are prepared in part or in total on the grill. For Quesadillas with Heirloom Tomatoes and Sweet Corn Salsa (page 69), only the corn is grilled. In the case of Grilled Pork Chops, Asian Pears, and Torpedo Onions (page 65), all of the cooking happens there.

Tomatoes (top) are to summer what strawberries are to spring. Heirloom varieties, nonhybrid plants cultivated by saving seeds from one crop to grow the next, are some of the most flavorful and juicy tomatoes available. Grilling defines summer cooking. Fresh corn (above) grills to a shiny bronze, developing a sweet, smoky flavor.

Autumn

Although the growing season is slowing down, farmers' markets in autumn are filled with a wide variety of fruits and vegetables. Apples (above) are a seasonal favorite, with many old varieties being revived. Root vegetables abound. Beets (right) are wonderfully colorful and far from ordinary these days, as farmers cultivate an exotic assortment.

Savoring Autumn

Autumn is the harvest season. Farmers' markets are filled with an abundance of produce that first sprang to light beneath the summer sun, reaching ripe perfection as the days draw in.

Winter squashes of every shape, size, and color crowd market stalls, including large, gray-green Hubbards; oval, pale yellow spaghetti squashes; reddish orange and green turbans shaped like their name implies; tan butternuts; and bright orange pumpkins ranging from tiny ones no bigger than a child's hand to huge specimens suitable for jack-o'-lanterns. The hard shells of all winter squashes give them excellent keeping qualities, making them ideal candidates for the pantry.

A wide variety of mushrooms, the sole offering of some market vendors, is available this time of year. Broccoli rabe and radishes are in season now, too. Artichokes return briefly for a second harvest. And the last of tender, early-season crops give way to their mature kin—fennel, potatoes, and root vegetables are good examples.

Autumn fruits provide that same sense of sustenance. Trees hang heavy with apples and pears. They show up in farmers' markets in sometimes bewildering variety. Be sure to ask individual vendors about the characteristics of each and which are best for eating out of hand or cooking. Persimmons and pomegranates are also available this time of year. The grape harvest that started in summer continues into autumn, with seedless table varieties such as Ruby and Thompson seedless easily found. Fresh dates and certain types of figs, particularly the sweet, purple-black Mission variety, are at their best now.

Among other seasonal specialties is a generous new crop of nuts, ready to add crunch and rich flavor to a variety of recipes.

As ocean waters grow cool, seafood stalls will begin to offer some shellfish and many excellent fresh and saltwater finfish. Turkey, duck, and game birds also appear, ready to grace holiday tables.

Cooking Slowly

As autumn days shorten and grow cool, we naturally gravitate toward the kitchen. The season's ingredients oblige us by requiring slow, gentle cooking to coax out their flavors, yielding dishes that warm and sustain.

This is the time of year for slowly simmering ingredients to make all manner of hearty soups and stews. The gentle, wet heat of the stew pot allows tough ingredients to become tender and flavorful while cooking without drying out. Braising, like stewing, depends on slow heat and liquid to get the job done. A braise, however, begins by first browning ingredients in a small amount of oil or butter and then calls for less liquid than a stew.

The rest of the process is the same. With the right sort of cooking vessel—a heavy-duty pot with a tight-fitting ovenproof lid—the job is made easy. You can brown the ingredients in batches on the stove top, add the liquid, cover, and then finish the cooking right on the burner or in the oven.

After months of trying to beat the summer heat, baking makes a comeback this time of year. Sweets such as Hachiya Persimmon Bar Cookies with Lemon Icing (page 86) capture the intense flavor of the season.

Stews are perfect autumn fare. The ingredients for Pork and Nopales Stew with Purslane and Cilantro (page 74) cook together slowly to yield a tender and tasty main dish.

Winter

Pears (above), first found in autumn, are available in abundance at the winter market. They lend themselves beautifully to baking (right) as evidenced by Tarte Tatin of Winter Pears (page 89), a delightful twist on the classic apple dessert.

Shopping in Winter

You might think that the shortest, coldest days of the year mean a barely stocked market. In truth, however, winter finds the earth yielding a generous variety of vegetables and fruits.

Many greens are robust enough to thrive in spite of cool temperatures, including members of the mustard family like kale and watercress; refreshingly bitter vegetables of the chicory family, including escarole (Batavian endive) and Belgian endive (chicory/witloof); and various cabbages and brussels sprouts. In all cases, look for young specimens with small leaves that are likely to be less bitter and more tender than older, larger ones.

Potatoes and root vegetables are at their most abundant in winter. Although many are harvested in autumn, they keep well in cold storage. Look for heavy-feeling, blemish-free specimens. And hard-shelled winter squashes, which first appeared in autumn, continue to be generously available through the cooler months.

In some locations, winter fruits seem to compensate for the season's grayness with their own bright bursts of sunshine. Harvested in the sunnier climes of Florida, California, and Texas,

citrus—oranges, tangerines, lemons, grapefruits, and various hybrids—join winter varieties of apples and pears in the market.

Your local farmers' market may also offer fruit and vegetable harvests of a different sort—dried or preserved produce. Look for stalls selling the latest crop of dried beans or dried fruits from summer. Some smart entrepreneurs will undoubtedly display jars of pickled cucumbers or tomatoes, or jams that capture the essence of the summer season's best and juiciest fruit.

With oceans icy cold, seafood stalls in large farmers' markets are likely to present the year's best selection of fresh shellfish, oysters, mussels and squid included. Prices should be excellent as well for roasting chickens and some cuts of pork and beef.

Leisurely Cooking

With the holiday and entertaining season comes cooking and spending more time in the kitchen. Having a stockpot on the stove and perhaps something sweet in the oven is a fine way to celebrate the foods of the season.

You'll find the robust fruits and vegetables of the winter market are well suited to leisurely cooking methods, from simmering and roasting to baking.

Long-simmered stews and braises of vegetables and meats carry over from autumn into the cool days of winter. Similarly, poaching should be considered for pome fruits such as apples, pears, and quinces, fresh or dried.

The dry heat of oven cooking also comes into play. Roasting is a particularly popular cooking method during the cold months, be it a slow process using moderate heat or a faster one using a high temperature. Roast Chicken Stuffed with Winter Savory and Preserved Lemons (page 81) is just one example of a fine seasonal centerpiece. Vegetables and fruits are good candidates for the roasting pan, too, the hot dry heat intensifying their flavors and colors.

Baking is yet another method associated with the season. A shell of tender pastry arguably does the best job of showing off the buttery flavor of winter pears or, in contrast, the tart nature of citrus.

TECHNIQUES

SHUCKING OYSTERS

Scrub the shell with a stiff-bristled brush under cold running water. Using a folded kitchen towel, grip an oyster, flat side up. Push in an oyster knife to one side of the hinge and pry upward.

Keeping the blade edge against the inside of the top shell, run the knife all around to sever the muscle holding the halves together. Cut beneath the oyster to detach it from the bottom shell.

Planning Menus

Once you've decided on the setting and nature of the meal, a casual supper or more formal affair, you can concentrate on the menu itself. As you flip through the pages that follow, you'll find many complementary dishes, from starters to desserts. The 10 sample menus presented here are meant to inspire, but, by all means, let the market be the ultimate guide: take advantage of the seasonal specialties that fill vendors' stalls, letting them shape the menu you serve.

Sophisticated Dinner

Spring Lettuces with Grapefruit
and Sautéed Scallops
PAGE 47

Steamed or Roasted
Salmon Fillet

Pomelo-Mint Sorbet
PAGE 104

Spring Fling

Sautéed Artichoke Hearts in
Parsley-Lemon Sauce
PAGE 33

Spring Wrap of Wild
Asparagus, Teleme Cheese,
and Chervil
PAGE 40

Meyer Lemon Tartlets
PAGE 90

Picnic Fare

Salad of Young Fennel,
Parmesan, and
Button Mushrooms
PAGE 39

Grilled Baby Leeks,
Green Garlic, and
Roast Lamb Sandwich
PAGE 55

Apricots and Cherries

Summertime Feast

Savory Yellow and Green
Zucchini Pancakes
PAGE 27

Linguine with Roasted Late-
Summer Tomato Sauce
PAGE 85

Peach Upside-Down Cake
PAGE 94

Mediterranean Repast

Feta Cheese, Kalamata Olives,
and Roasted Red Peppers

Roast Chicken Stuffed
with Winter Savory and
Preserved Lemons
PAGE 81

Figs and Walnuts

Springtime Glory

Fresh Pea Soup
with Chive Blossom Cream
PAGE 36

Pan-Seared Halibut
with Sautéed Baby Vegetables
PAGE 62

Strawberries and Cream

Asian Sampler

Japanese Cucumbers with
Soy-Sesame Dressing
PAGE 59

Spicy Black Bean Beef with
Thai Basil and Jasmine Rice
PAGE 78

Satsuma Mandarin and
Star Anise Compote
PAGE 93

Cool-Weather Supper

Salad of Winter Greens

Penne with Sautéed Radicchio,
Fennel, and Prosciutto
PAGE 73

Hachiya Persimmon Bar
Cookies with Lemon Icing
PAGE 86

Mexican Flavors

Pork and Nopales Stew
with Purslane and Cilantro
PAGE 74

Grilled Corn Tortillas

Papaya with Lime Juice

Harvest Menu

Salt-Roasted Mussels with
Pimiento Dipping Sauce
PAGE 24

Terrine of Winter Kale
and Yukon Gold Potatoes
with Sausage
PAGE 66

Tarte Tatin of Winter Pears
PAGE 89

Oysters with Fresh Horseradish

PREP TIME: 55 MINUTES

INGREDIENTS

4 dozen oysters, well scrubbed

1 horseradish root, about ½ lb (250 g)

¼ cup (2 fl oz/60 ml) heavy (double) cream (optional)

1 lemon, cut into wedges (optional)

SERVING TIP: To hold shucked oysters steady on their serving trays or plates, nestle them into beds of crushed ice or rock salt.

Fresh horseradish has a fiery potency that marries well with raw oysters. Both oysters and horseradish are in season in the cooler months and can be found at many farmers' markets. Use the horseradish immediately upon grating it, as its power diminishes the longer the volatile oils are exposed to the air. To speed up the shucking, be sure to have extra oyster knives on hand so your guests can assist you.

SERVES 4

❋ Grip an oyster, flat side up, with a folded kitchen towel. Push in the tip of an oyster knife to one side of the hinge located on the narrow end and pry upward to open the shell. Run the knife blade all along the inside of the top shell to sever the muscle that joins the shells. Discard the top shell. Then carefully run the knife underneath the oyster to detach it from the bottom shell. Try not to lose any of the flavorful juices in the shell. Arrange the oysters in their bottom shells on trays or individual plates. Refrigerate until serving.

❋ Using a knife or vegetable peeler, peel away the dark, rough skin from the horseradish. On the small holes of a handheld grater, grate enough of the root to measure about 1 cup (5 oz/155 g). Transfer the horseradish to a small serving bowl. To make a sauce, add the cream and stir well.

❋ Serve the oysters on the half shell with the sauce and the lemon wedges alongside. Encourage guests to spoon about 1 teaspoon sauce onto each oyster before eating.

NUTRITIONAL ANALYSIS PER SERVING: Calories 148 (Kilojoules 622); Protein 13 g; Carbohydrates 14 g; Total Fat 4 g; Saturated Fat 1 g; Cholesterol 94 mg; Sodium 193 mg; Dietary Fiber 0 g

Roasted Root Vegetables in Filo Packets

PREP TIME: 45 MINUTES, PLUS
1 HOUR FOR MARINATING

COOKING TIME: 1½ HOURS,
PLUS 30 MINUTES FOR
COOLING VEGETABLES

INGREDIENTS

1 large fennel bulb, about 1 lb (500 g)

6 young carrots, about 1 lb (500 g) total weight, peeled and cut into 1-inch (2.5-cm) cubes

3 parsnips, about 1½ lb (750 g) total weight, peeled and cut into 1-inch (2.5-cm) cubes

3 leeks, about 2 lb (1 kg) total weight, halved lengthwise and cut into slices ½ inch (12 mm) thick

4 potatoes such as Red Rose, Yukon gold, or Yellow Finn, about ¾ lb (375 g) total weight, unpeeled, cut into 1-inch (2.5-cm) cubes

4 turnips, about 1 lb (500 g) total weight, peeled and cut into 1-inch (2.5-cm) cubes

1 yellow onion, about ½ lb (250 g), cut into ½-inch (12-mm) dice

½ cup (4 fl oz/125 ml) extra-virgin olive oil

8 fresh thyme sprigs, plus sprigs for garnish

8 fresh winter savory or 4 fresh rosemary sprigs

1 teaspoon salt

2 teaspoons ground pepper

24 sheets filo dough, thawed if frozen

2 oz (60 g) fresh goat cheese

¼ cup (2 oz/60 g) unsalted butter, melted

Farmers' markets in winter abound with root vegetables of all kinds. An elegant and easy way to prepare them is wrapped in filo dough with just a taste of goat cheese.

MAKES 12 PACKETS; SERVES 6–8

❀ Cut off the stems, feathery tops, and any bruised outer stalks from the fennel bulb. Cut the bulb into ½-inch (12-mm) cubes. Place in a large bowl. Add the carrots, parsnips, leeks, potatoes, turnips, and onion. Pour the olive oil over the vegetables, add the 8 thyme sprigs and the winter savory or rosemary sprigs, and sprinkle with the salt and pepper. Toss gently to coat well. Let stand for 1 hour at room temperature, turning from time to time.

❀ Preheat an oven to 350°F (180°C).

❀ Using a slotted spoon, transfer the vegetables to a baking sheet and spread them out in a single layer. (Use 2 baking sheets, if necessary.) Reserve the olive oil left behind in the bowl for basting. Roast, turning every 15 minutes or so and basting with the reserved oil, until soft and tender, about 1 hour. Remove from the oven and let cool completely, about 30 minutes. Discard the herb sprigs.

❀ Line 2 baking sheets with parchment (baking) paper. Cut the filo sheets in half crosswise. Working with a half sheet at a time, place on a work surface; keep the other sheets covered with a damp kitchen towel. Put ⅓–½ cup (2–3 oz/60–90 g) roasted root vegetables in the center of the sheet and dot with a scant 1 tablespoon of the goat cheese. Fold in each side over the filling, then fold in the open ends, forming a square. Brush the square with melted butter and place, folded side down, in the center of another half sheet. Wrap again in the same way, then brush the square with melted butter. Place, folded side down, on yet another half sheet, wrap, and brush again with the melted butter. Repeat a fourth time and again brush with melted butter. Place on the lined baking sheet. Repeat with the remaining ingredients to make a total of 12 packets.

❀ Bake until the filo is golden brown and crisp, about 25 minutes.

❀ Transfer the packets to a platter. Garnish with herb sprigs and serve immediately.

NUTRITIONAL ANALYSIS PER PACKET: Calories 358 (Kilojoules 1,504); Protein 6 g; Carbohydrates 47 g; Total Fat 17 g; Saturated Fat 5 g; Cholesterol 13 mg; Sodium 473 mg; Dietary Fiber 6 g

Creamy Butternut Squash with Fruit Chutney

PREP TIME: 15 MINUTES

COOKING TIME: 2½ HOURS

INGREDIENTS

1 butternut squash, about 3 lb
(1.5 kg)

FOR THE CHUTNEY

1½ lb (750 g) peaches, peeled, pitted,
and coarsely chopped

½ lb (250 g) plums, halved, pitted,
and coarsely chopped

½ lb (250 g) seedless grapes, stems
removed

2 yellow onions, chopped

1¾ cups (13 oz/410 g) firmly packed
brown sugar

1 cup (6 oz/185 g) dried currants or
raisins

¼ cup (1¼ oz/37 g) peeled and finely
chopped fresh ginger

4 cloves garlic, minced

1 teaspoon cayenne pepper

1½ cups (12 fl oz/375 ml) apple
cider vinegar

3 cinnamon sticks

1 tablespoon peppercorns

1 tablespoon whole cloves

2 tablespoons unsalted butter

¼ teaspoon salt

The butternut is one of early autumn's most dense-fleshed, flavorful squashes. Its nutty flavor adapts to both sweet and savory preparations. It pairs well with a sweet-tart chutney made from late-summer fruits.

SERVES 4

❀ Preheat an oven to 350°F (180°C).

❀ Using a sharp knife, puncture the squash in 4 or 5 places. Put the squash on a baking sheet. Bake until it is thoroughly tender and can be easily pierced to the center with the knife, 2–2½ hours.

❀ Meanwhile, make the chutney: In a heavy nonaluminum saucepan, combine the peaches, plums, grapes, onions, brown sugar, currants or raisins, ginger, garlic, cayenne pepper, and vinegar. Place the cinnamon sticks, peppercorns, and cloves on a square of cheesecloth (muslin) and tie the corners securely with kitchen string. Add to the saucepan. Bring to a boil over high heat, stirring often. Reduce the heat to low and simmer uncovered, stirring occasionally, until the mixture develops a somewhat loose, jamlike consistency, 50–60 minutes. When it begins to thicken, during the last 10–15 minutes of cooking, stir often with a wooden spoon to prevent burning. Remove from the heat and let cool to room temperature. Discard the cheesecloth bag. You will need about ½ cup (5 oz/155 g) of the chutney; reserve the remainder for another use. It will keep tightly covered in the refrigerator for up to 2 months.

❀ Remove the squash from the oven and let cool for about 10 minutes. Using a large, sharp knife and steadying the squash with a hand well protected by an oven glove, cut the squash in half lengthwise. Using a large spoon, scoop out and discard the seeds. Then scoop out the hot flesh and put it in a warmed bowl. Add the 2 tablespoons butter and the salt. Stir until the butter has melted and the squash is creamy.

❀ Butter the inside of a round biscuit cutter 4 inches (10 cm) in diameter and 1½ inches (4 cm) deep. Place on a warmed individual plate. Fill it to the brim with the hot squash, then lift the cutter straight up, leaving a tidy round of squash. Make 3 more molds on 3 additional plates.

❀ Place 2 tablespoons chutney on top of each squash round and serve.

NUTRITIONAL ANALYSIS PER SERVING: Calories 247 (Kilojoules 1,037); Protein 3 g; Carbohydrates 47 g; Total Fat 8 g; Saturated Fat 5 g; Cholesterol 21 mg; Sodium 159 mg; Dietary Fiber 5 g

Salt-Roasted Mussels with Pimiento Dipping Sauce

PREP TIME: 10 MINUTES

COOKING TIME: 10 MINUTES,
   PLUS 15 MINUTES FOR
   HEATING SALT

INGREDIENTS

2 pimiento peppers

3 cloves garlic

1 tablespoon extra-virgin olive oil

1 teaspoon lemon juice

¼ teaspoon salt

¼ teaspoon ground pepper

2 tablespoons mayonnaise

rock salt for roasting

1 lb (500 g) mussels, well scrubbed
   and debearded

COOKING TIP: If you'd like a spicy
sauce, add ¼–½ teaspoon cayenne
pepper to the sauce with the salt.

Mussels and other shellfish can be found at many farmers' markets, especially with the increase in the number of different types being farmed. Pimientos, late-maturing sweet peppers usually available in autumn and into winter, make an excellent dipping sauce for the hot shellfish. If unavailable, substitute thick, meaty red bell peppers (capsicums).

SERVES 4

⚘ Preheat a broiler (griller).

⚘ To make the sauce, cut the pimientos in half lengthwise and remove the stems, seeds, and ribs. Place, cut sides down, on a baking sheet. Broil (grill) until the skins blacken and blister. Remove from the broiler, drape the peppers loosely with aluminum foil, and let cool for 10 minutes. Using your fingers or a small knife, peel away the skins.

⚘ Preheat an oven to 500°F (260°C).

⚘ In a small food processor or a blender, combine the garlic, olive oil, lemon juice, salt, and pepper. Process until smooth. Add the roasted peppers and process until smooth. Transfer the purée to a small bowl. Add the mayonnaise and stir until well blended. You should have about ½ cup (4 fl oz/125 ml). Set aside until serving. The flavors will intensify as the mixture stands.

⚘ In a heavy ovenproof frying pan or baking dish, make a bed of rock salt about 1½ inches (4 cm) deep. Place in the oven for 15 minutes to heat the salt thoroughly. Discard any mussels that do not close to the touch. Remove the pan or dish from the oven and arrange the mussels in a single layer on the salt. Return it to the oven and roast just until the mussels open, 5–7 minutes. Discard any that did not open.

⚘ Remove from the oven and transfer the mussels to a platter, or bring the pan or baking dish to the table. If you do the latter, be careful, as the vessel and the salt are extremely hot. Divide the dipping sauce among small individual bowls and serve alongside.

NUTRITIONAL ANALYSIS PER SERVING: Calories 122 (Kilojoules 512); Protein 4 g; Carbohydrates 5 g; Total Fat 10 g; Saturated Fat 1 g; Cholesterol 13 mg; Sodium 278 mg; Dietary Fiber 1 g

Savory Yellow and Green Zucchini Pancakes

PREP TIME: 20 MINUTES

COOKING TIME: 20 MINUTES

INGREDIENTS

4 yellow zucchini (courgettes)

4 green zucchini (courgettes)

½ yellow onion

½ teaspoon salt

1 egg, lightly beaten

2 cloves garlic, minced

1 tablespoon all-purpose (plain) flour

1 tablespoon chopped fresh marjoram

½ teaspoon ground pepper

1–2 tablespoons vegetable oil

Delicate and soft, these pancakes have a texture and flavor reminiscent of puréed squash. Choose zucchini with thin skins, as thicker-skinned ones may have a bitter taste that will not sufficiently mellow during the brief cooking time.

MAKES ABOUT 12 PANCAKES; SERVES 4

❀ Trim all the zucchini, but do not peel. Shred the zucchini, then the onion. In a bowl, toss the shredded zucchini with the salt. Let stand for 5 minutes. Using your hands, squeeze the zucchini to remove excess liquid. Add the onion, egg, garlic, flour, marjoram, and pepper to the zucchini. Mix well.

❀ Pour about 1 tablespoon vegetable oil into the bottom of a large frying pan to form a thin film, and place over medium-high heat. When the pan is hot, working in batches, drop in the squash mixture, using a heaping tablespoonful for each pancake. Using the back of a spoon, press on the top of each spoonful to form a pancake a scant ½ inch (12 mm) thick. Fry until golden brown on the underside, 3–4 minutes. Turn and continue to fry until golden brown on the second side, 2–3 minutes longer. Transfer to a warmed platter and keep warm. Repeat until all the squash mixture is used, adding more oil to the pan as needed.

❀ Serve the pancakes hot.

NUTRITIONAL ANALYSIS PER SERVING: Calories 114 (Kilojoules 479); Protein 5 g; Carbohydrates 11 g; Total Fat 7 g; Saturated Fat 1 g; Cholesterol 53 mg; Sodium 313 mg; Dietary Fiber 2 g

Roasted Figs with Rosemary, Goat Cheese, and Pancetta

PREP TIME: 15 MINUTES

COOKING TIME: 15 MINUTES

INGREDIENTS

12 soft, ripe Mission figs

¼ lb (125 g) fresh goat cheese

1 teaspoon minced fresh rosemary, plus sprigs for garnish

½ teaspoon ground pepper

¼ lb (125 g) pancetta or bacon, thinly sliced

MAKE-AHEAD TIP: The stuffed figs may be completely assembled, covered, and refrigerated several hours in advance. Bring to room temperature, then roast just before serving.

In temperate climates, figs come into season twice a year, once in early summer and again in autumn, presenting two opportunities to prepare fig-based dishes. Black Mission figs are among the most readily available. Their sweetness, combined with the tartness of the cheese and the saltiness of the pancetta, delivers a complexity of intense and satisfying flavors. Choose figs that are very soft, a sign that their sugar content has developed.

SERVES 4

❋ Preheat an oven to 400°F (200°C).

❋ Cut a slit in each fig from the stem end to the base, slicing about three-fourths of the way through. Set aside.

❋ In a bowl, combine the goat cheese, minced rosemary, and pepper. Stir until blended. Cut the pancetta or bacon slices into pieces 4 inches (10 cm) long, or just long enough to wrap around a fig once it is filled, plus a 1-inch (2.5-cm) overlap.

❋ Put a spoonful of the cheese mixture inside each fig, wrap the fig with a length of pancetta or bacon, and fasten in place with a toothpick. Place the figs on an ungreased baking sheet. Roast until the pancetta or bacon is browned, the surface of the figs is shiny, and the cheese is nearly melted, 10–15 minutes. If the cheese is nearly melted but the pancetta or bacon has not yet browned, place the figs under a hot broiler (griller) for a minute or two.

❋ Transfer the figs to a warmed platter or individual plates. Garnish with rosemary sprigs and serve hot.

NUTRITIONAL ANALYSIS PER SERVING: Calories 256 (Kilojoules 1,075); Protein 12 g; Carbohydrates 29 g; Total Fat 11 g; Saturated Fat 6 g; Cholesterol 27 mg; Sodium 432 mg; Dietary Fiber 5 g

Bruschetta with Eggplant Caviar

PREP TIME: 20 MINUTES

COOKING TIME: 1¼ HOURS

INGREDIENTS

I large globe eggplant (aubergine), about I lb (500 g)

FOR THE BAGUETTE TOASTS

2 baguettes, each cut on the diagonal into slices ½ inch (12 mm) thick

¼ cup (2 fl oz/60 ml) extra-virgin olive oil

4 cloves garlic

2 tomatoes, peeled and chopped

½ yellow onion, coarsely chopped

2 cloves garlic, coarsely chopped

I tablespoon extra-virgin olive oil

½ cup (2½ oz/75 g) pitted and coarsely chopped Kalamata olives

¼ cup (⅓ oz/10 g) coarsely chopped fresh cilantro (fresh coriander)

I–1½ tablespoons lemon juice

I teaspoon salt

I teaspoon ground pepper

MAKE-AHEAD TIP: The eggplant can be baked I day in advance, allowed to cool, wrapped in plastic wrap, and refrigerated. Combine with the other ingredients the day of serving.

Eggplant caviar is a wonderful spread to make when eggplants are plentiful in summer. The bruschetta can be served already assembled for a casual occasion. For a more formal gathering, present each diner with an individual ramekin of caviar and a plate of the toasted baguette slices to make their own.

MAKES 48 TOASTS

❁ Preheat an oven to 300°F (150°C). Place the eggplant on a baking sheet. Bake until very soft and tender when pierced with a knife and the meat pulls away from the browned skin, about 1¼ hours. Remove from the oven and let cool.

❁ While the eggplant is cooling, prepare the toasts: Raise the oven temperature to 400°F (200°C). Place the baguette slices on baking sheets and drizzle them evenly with the olive oil. Bake until golden on top, about 15 minutes. Remove from the oven, turn over the slices, and return to the oven. Continue to bake until golden on the second side, about 5 minutes longer. Remove from the oven. When the toasts are cool enough to handle, rub the most golden side of each one with a whole garlic clove.

❁ When the eggplant is cool enough to handle, peel it and coarsely chop the flesh. Set aside. In a blender or food processor, combine the tomatoes, onion, garlic, and olive oil. Process until smooth. Add the eggplant, olives, cilantro, lemon juice to taste, salt, and pepper. Process until smooth. You should have about 3 cups (27 oz/845 g).

❁ To serve, spread each toast with about 1 tablespoon of the eggplant caviar and arrange on 1 or 2 platters or on individual serving plates.

NUTRITIONAL ANALYSIS PER TOAST: Calories 47 (Kilojoules 197); Protein 1 g; Carbohydrates 6 g; Total Fat 2 g; Saturated Fat 0 g; Cholesterol 0 mg; Sodium 134 mg; Dietary Fiber 0 g

Sautéed Artichoke Hearts in Parsley-Lemon Sauce

PREP TIME: 20 MINUTES

COOKING TIME: 15 MINUTES

INGREDIENTS

2 lemons

6 artichokes

3 tablespoons extra-virgin olive oil

1 clove garlic, minced

⅓ cup (3 fl oz/80 ml) lemon juice

⅓ cup (3 fl oz/80 ml) chicken or
vegetable broth

½ teaspoon salt

2 tablespoons minced fresh flat-leaf
(Italian) parsley

PREP TIP: Use a sharp stainless-steel knife to trim the artichokes and a stainless-steel spoon to scoop out the choke. Other materials can cause the cut portions to discolor.

Artichokes have a flush in the spring and then again in autumn. The autumn specimens are more open and often have a tinge of brown, or a "kiss of frost" as growers call it, which does not at all detract from their flavor.

SERVES 4

❊ Have ready a large bowl of water. Cut 1 of the lemons in half and squeeze the juice into the water. Working with 1 artichoke at a time, cut off the stem near the base. Peel back and snap off the first 1 or 2 layers of leaves, then cut off the top third of the artichoke. Starting at the base, break off the tough outer leaves, snapping them downward, until you reach the tender, pale green inner leaves. Cut off the uppermost part of the artichoke again, leaving about 1 inch (2.5 cm) of leaves rising. Trim around the base to make a smooth surface, then cut the artichoke in half lengthwise. If the center choke has developed any prickly tips, scoop it out with the edge of a spoon. If the choke is only furry, leave it, as it will be edible once cooked. Cut each half lengthwise into 4 pieces, and drop them into the lemon water. Repeat with the remaining artichokes. When all the artichokes are trimmed, drain and pat dry.

❊ In a heavy-bottomed saucepan over medium heat, warm the olive oil. Add the garlic and the artichokes and sauté until the artichokes turn lightly golden, 4–5 minutes. Raise the heat to high, add the lemon juice, and deglaze the pan, stirring to dislodge any browned bits from the pan bottom. Then add the broth and salt, reduce the heat to low, cover, and simmer until the bases of the artichoke pieces are easily pierced with a fork, about 10 minutes.

❊ Stir in the parsley and remove the pan from the heat. Using a slotted spoon, transfer the artichoke pieces to warmed individual plates or a serving platter or bowl. Spoon the pan sauce over the top. Cut the remaining lemon into slices and garnish the artichokes. Serve hot or at room temperature.

NUTRITIONAL ANALYSIS PER SERVING: Calories 283 (Kilojoules 1,189); Protein 7 g; Carbohydrates 25 g; Total Fat 21 g; Saturated Fat 3 g; Cholesterol 0 mg; Sodium 549 mg; Dietary Fiber 7 g

Mixed Greens with Panfried Goat Cheese and Golden Beets

PREP TIME: 20 MINUTES

COOKING TIME: 35 MINUTES

INGREDIENTS

5 or 6 small golden beets with greens
 intact, each about 1 inch (2.5 cm)
 in diameter

¾ teaspoon salt

¼ lb (125 g) fresh goat cheese

½ cup (2 oz/60 g) unseasoned
 medium-fine dried bread crumbs

½ teaspoon fresh thyme leaves

½ teaspoon ground pepper

FOR THE VINAIGRETTE
⅓ cup (3 fl oz/80 ml) extra-virgin
 olive oil

2 tablespoons red wine vinegar

½ teaspoon salt

½ teaspoon ground pepper

2 cups (2 oz/60 g) frisée leaves,
 interior pale yellow leaves only

2 cups (2 oz/60 g) baby spinach
 leaves

1 tablespoon extra-virgin olive oil

MAKE-AHEAD TIP: The beets can be
cooked, peeled, and diced up to 1 day
in advance.

You can buy everything you need for this salad at the farmers'
market from early summer through autumn, the best time of
the year for fresh goat cheese.

SERVES 4

❀ Trim off the greens from each beet, cutting to within ½ inch (12 mm)
of the crown. Choose the nicest, smallest, most tender greens to add to
the salad and set aside.

❀ In a saucepan, combine the beets with water to cover by 2 inches
(5 cm). Add ½ teaspoon of the salt and bring to a boil over medium-high
heat. Reduce the heat to low, cover, and simmer until tender, about
30 minutes. Remove from the heat and drain. When cool enough to
handle, peel the beets and cut into ¼-inch (6-mm) dice. Set aside.

❀ Divide the cheese into 4 equal portions. Shape each portion into
a patty about 3 inches (7.5 cm) in diameter. (If you have purchased a
log-shaped cheese, cut it into slices ¾ inch/2 cm thick.) In a bowl, mix
together the bread crumbs, thyme, pepper, and the remaining ¼ teaspoon
salt. Pour the mixture onto a sheet of waxed paper. One at a time, press
both sides of each cheese patty into the mixture. Set aside.

❀ To make the vinaigrette, in the bottom of a large salad bowl, stir
together the olive oil, vinegar, salt, and pepper with a fork.

❀ Add the frisée, spinach, and the reserved beet greens to the salad
bowl and toss to coat well. Divide among individual plates and set aside.

❀ In a frying pan, warm the olive oil over medium heat. Add the patties
and cook until lightly browned on the underside, 1–2 minutes. Turn and
continue to cook until the cheese begins to spread slightly, about 1 minute
longer. Slip a spatula under each patty and place it on a plate of dressed
greens. Sprinkle with the diced beets and serve immediately.

NUTRITIONAL ANALYSIS PER SERVING: Calories 347 (Kilojoules 1,457); Protein 9 g;
Carbohydrates 16 g; Total Fat 29 g; Saturated Fat 7 g; Cholesterol 13 mg; Sodium 1,035 mg;
Dietary Fiber 2 g

Fresh Pea Soup with Chive Blossom Cream

PREP TIME: 15 MINUTES,
PLUS 30 MINUTES FOR
STEEPING CREAM

COOKING TIME: 25 MINUTES

INGREDIENTS

6 fresh chive blossoms

1 cup (8 fl oz/250 ml) heavy (double)
cream

3 cups (24 fl oz/750 ml) low-sodium
chicken broth

2 lb (1 kg) English peas, shelled

1 teaspoon salt

½ teaspoon ground white pepper

COOKING TIP: Late-season peas,
which have a higher starch content
than their early-season kin, make
the creamiest soup.

English peas come into season at the same time chives are putting forth their delicate onion-flavored blossoms, and market vendors often sell chives with their blossoms intact. For a festive brunch, serve the soup with poppy-seed rolls and an array of fresh fruit.

SERVES 4

❊ In a small saucepan over medium-high heat, combine 3 of the chive blossoms and the cream. Bring to a boil, reduce the heat to low, and simmer, uncovered, until the cream thickens and is reduced by nearly half, 4–5 minutes. Remove from the heat and let stand for 30 minutes to allow the flavors to develop.

❊ Separate the petals from the remaining 3 blossoms. Mince the petals and set them aside.

❊ In a saucepan over medium-high heat, combine the chicken broth, peas, salt, and pepper. Bring to a boil, reduce the heat to low, and simmer until the peas are soft, 10–20 minutes. The timing will depend upon the size and maturity of the peas.

❊ Remove from the heat and let cool slightly. Transfer to a blender or food processor and purée until smooth. Return the purée to the saucepan, place over medium heat, and heat to serving temperature.

❊ Meanwhile, remove the whole chive blossoms from the cream and discard. Reheat the cream over medium heat until it is quite hot.

❊ To serve, ladle the soup into warmed individual bowls. Add a spoonful of the cream to each serving and garnish with the minced petals. Serve immediately.

NUTRITIONAL ANALYSIS PER SERVING: Calories 299 (Kilojoules 1,256); Protein 8 g; Carbohydrates 15 g; Total Fat 23 g; Saturated Fat 14 g; Cholesterol 84 mg; Sodium 688 mg; Dietary Fiber 3 g

Salad of Young Fennel, Parmesan, and Button Mushrooms

PREP TIME: 15 MINUTES

INGREDIENTS

I young, tender fennel bulb

½ lb (250 g) firm fresh button
mushrooms, brushed clean

3 tablespoons lemon juice

1½ tablespoons extra-virgin olive oil

I tablespoon chopped fresh flat-leaf
(Italian) parsley

½ teaspoon salt

½ teaspoon ground pepper

8 large, attractive butter (Boston)
lettuce leaves

wedge Italian Parmesan cheese

Try making this Italian salad in early summer or autumn, when the first of the season's fennel—its flavor mild and true, its flesh crisp—appears in farmers' markets. Look for mushrooms that are very firm with caps tightly fastened to the stems.

SERVES 4

❀ Cut off the stems, feathery tops, and bruised outer stalks from the fennel bulb. Using a mandoline or sharp knife, cut crosswise into paper-thin slices. You should have about 2 cups (8 oz/250 g). Place in a bowl.

❀ Trim the stem from each mushroom to make a clean, flat surface, then cut the mushrooms into paper-thin slices. Add to the fennel along with the lemon juice, olive oil, parsley, salt, and pepper. Toss gently to coat evenly.

❀ Divide the lettuce leaves evenly among 4 individual plates, making a bed on each plate. Then divide the fennel and mushroom mixture evenly among the plates. Using a vegetable peeler, cheese plane, or very sharp knife, shave 4 or 5 pieces of Parmesan from the cheese wedge directly onto each plate. You will need about 2 oz (60 g) total for the shavings. Serve at once.

NUTRITIONAL ANALYSIS PER SERVING: Calories 130 (Kilojoules 546); Protein 7 g; Carbohydrates 6 g; Total Fat 9 g; Saturated Fat 3 g; Cholesterol 10 mg; Sodium 579 mg; Dietary Fiber 2 g

Spring Wrap of Wild Asparagus, Teleme Cheese, and Chervil

PREP TIME: 10 MINUTES

COOKING TIME: 25 MINUTES

INGREDIENTS

12 thin asparagus spears

1 teaspoon canola or other light oil, or as needed

6 flour tortillas, each 8 inches (20 cm) in diameter

3 oz (90 g) teleme cheese, thinly sliced

¼ cup (⅓ oz/10 g) chopped fresh chervil

In early spring, wild asparagus shoots start appearing. They are no larger than a pencil, very tender, and sweet. If wild spears are not available at your farmers' market, choose cultivated asparagus of the same size for this quick-to-fix wrap. Teleme is a mild-flavored, soft cow's milk cheese coated in rice flour. If you're not able to find it, fontina or Brie could be used instead. If chervil proves difficult to find, use tarragon or flat-leaf (Italian) parsley instead.

SERVES 6

❁ Bend each asparagus spear near the cut end until it snaps. Discard the tough bit of stalk. Place the spears on a steamer rack over boiling water, cover, and steam until just barely tender when pierced with the tip of a sharp knife, 3–4 minutes. Transfer to a plate.

❁ In a frying pan over medium heat, warm the oil. When it is hot, lay 1 tortilla in the pan. Place 2 or 3 slices of cheese down the center and cook until the edges of the tortilla begin to curl and the cheese begins to melt, 2–3 minutes. Place 2 asparagus spears down the center on top of the cheese and sprinkle with about 2 teaspoons of the chervil. Using tongs, transfer to a plate. Carefully roll up the tortilla to form a cylinder, and place, seam side down, on a platter or on individual plates. Keep warm. Repeat until all the tortillas are used, adding more oil to the pan if necessary.

❁ Serve the filled tortillas hot.

NUTRITIONAL ANALYSIS PER SERVING: Calories 166 (Kilojoules 697); Protein 6 g; Carbohydrates 20 g; Total Fat 7 g; Saturated Fat 2 g; Cholesterol 5 mg; Sodium 238 mg; Dietary Fiber 1 g

Fresh Cranberry Beans, Broccoli Rabe, and Pancetta Salad

PREP TIME: 15 MINUTES

COOKING TIME: 25 MINUTES

INGREDIENTS

1½–2 lb (750 g–1 kg) fresh cranberry (borlotti) beans or other fresh shelling beans

¾ teaspoon salt

1 bay leaf

2 fresh winter savory or thyme sprigs

1 lb (500 g) broccoli rabe

⅓ cup (3 fl oz/80 ml) extra-virgin olive oil

2 cloves garlic, minced

½ teaspoon ground pepper

¼ lb (125 g) pancetta, thinly sliced and cut into 1-inch (2.5-cm) pieces

3–4 tablespoons red wine vinegar

PREP TIP: To determine the maturity of a cranberry bean or any other shelling bean (podded beans that are eaten fresh), bite through a raw one. If your teeth meet no resistance, the bean is young and tender and will cook quickly. If the bean has begun to harden, you will meet with resistance. These beans are more mature and will take longer to cook.

Cranberry beans, distinguished by their red-and-white coloring, are at the market in summer. Broccoli rabe (also known as broccoli raab and rapini) is also available at this time. Unlike broccoli, it's at its peak of flavor when you can see a bit of yellow in the buds and a few flowers are open. The delightfully bitter taste provides an appealing counterpoint to the soft, sweet taste of the cranberry beans and the salty bits of Italian bacon.

SERVES 4

✺ Shell the beans; you should have about 1 cup (6 oz/185 g). Place them in a saucepan with water to cover by 2 inches (5 cm). Add ½ teaspoon of the salt, the bay leaf, and the winter savory or thyme and bring to a boil over high heat. Reduce the heat to medium and cook, uncovered, until tender, 15–25 minutes. The cooking time will depend upon the maturity of the beans; older beans will take longer to cook.

✺ Meanwhile, remove any tough stems from the broccoli rabe and discard. Chop the tender portions; you should have about 2 cups (6 oz/185 g). When the beans are almost done, in a frying pan over medium-high heat, warm the olive oil. When it is hot, add the garlic and sauté until translucent, 2–3 minutes. Add the broccoli rabe and sprinkle with the remaining ¼ teaspoon salt and the pepper. Cook, stirring often, until the greens change color and are tender to the bite, 4–5 minutes. Remove from the heat and cover to keep warm. Set aside.

✺ At the same time, in a small frying pan, cook the pancetta until the fat is translucent, 3–4 minutes.

✺ Drain the beans and place in a warmed serving bowl. Add the broccoli rabe and the pancetta with any of its rendered fat. Then add the vinegar to taste and toss to mix well. Serve immediately.

NUTRITIONAL ANALYSIS PER SERVING: Calories 321 (Kilojoules 1,348); Protein 9 g; Carbohydrates 11 g; Total Fat 27 g; Saturated Fat 6 g; Cholesterol 17 mg; Sodium 775 mg; Dietary Fiber 3 g

Italian Sausage Sandwich with Sautéed Onions and Peppers

PREP TIME: 15 MINUTES

COOKING TIME: 30 MINUTES

INGREDIENTS

6 hot or sweet Italian sausages, about 1½ lb (750 g) total weight

2 tablespoons olive oil

2 large, red (Spanish) onions, thinly sliced

4 long, green Italian sweet peppers (capsicums), seeded and cut into thin rounds

2 red bell peppers (capsicums), seeded and cut lengthwise into strips ¼ inch (6 mm) wide

1 orange bell pepper (capsicum), seeded and cut lengthwise into strips ¼ inch (6 mm) wide

2 tablespoons balsamic vinegar

4 sourdough or other sandwich rolls, split and toasted

2 tablespoons Dijon mustard

Make this hearty sandwich during summer and autumn when farmers' markets are ablaze with different colors and varieties of sweet peppers. Serve with a tossed green salad for a satisfying lunch or dinner.

SERVES 4

❀ Cut each sausage in half lengthwise. In a large frying pan over medium heat, fry the sausages, turning once, until crisp and cooked through, 4–5 minutes on each side. Remove from the heat and keep warm while you prepare the onions and peppers.

❀ In a frying pan over medium-high heat, warm the oil. When the oil is hot, add the onions and cook them, scraping and turning them often with a spatula, until limp and slightly browned, 7–8 minutes. Transfer to a bowl and keep warm.

❀ Cook the green, red, and orange peppers the same way until they are limp and browned on the edges, about 10 minutes. Add the balsamic vinegar and deglaze the pan, stirring to dislodge any browned bits from the pan bottom, 1–2 minutes longer.

❀ To make the sandwiches, lightly spread the cut sides of the toasted rolls with the mustard. Divide the onions, the pepper mixture, and the sausage halves evenly among them, allowing 3 pieces of sausage for each sandwich. Close the sandwiches.

❀ Cut the sandwiches in half and serve hot.

NUTRITIONAL ANALYSIS PER SERVING: Calories 706 (Kilojoules 2,965); Protein 33 g; Carbohydrates 50 g; Total Fat 41 g; Saturated Fat 13 g; Cholesterol 97 mg; Sodium 1,688 mg; Dietary Fiber 5 g

Spring Lettuces with Grapefruit and Sautéed Scallops

INGREDIENTS

1 grapefruit

juice of 1 grapefruit (about ½ cup/
4 fl oz/125 ml)

1 tablespoon extra-virgin olive oil

2 tablespoons minced fresh tarragon,
plus 4 sprigs for garnish

1 teaspoon minced shallot

¾ teaspoon salt

4 cups (4 oz/125 g) mixed young,
tender lettuces

12 sea scallops (about ¾ lb/375 g)

1 tablespoon unsalted butter

½ teaspoon ground pepper

SERVING TIP: Double the quantities
to make a satisfying yet light main-
course salad.

The tart, sweet taste of grapefruits is a refreshing counterpoint
to the sweetness of plump scallops. Tarragon, with its own
citrusy tones, is the ideal complement to the two flavors.

SERVES 4

❀ Using a small, sharp knife, cut a slice off the top and bottom of the
grapefruit to expose the flesh. Place the fruit upright on the cutting
board and thickly slice off the peel in strips, cutting around the contour
of the fruit to expose the flesh. Holding the grapefruit over a bowl, cut
along either side of each section, letting the sections drop into the bowl.
Remove any seeds and discard. Cut the sections into ½-inch (12-mm)
pieces. Set them aside.

❀ Pour half of the grapefruit juice into a large bowl and add the olive
oil, minced tarragon, shallot, and ½ teaspoon of the salt. Using a fork or
spoon, mix well. Add the lettuces and the grapefruit pieces to the bowl
and toss to mix well. Divide the mixture evenly among individual plates.

❀ Pat the scallops dry with paper towels. In a frying pan over medium-
high heat, melt the butter. When it is foaming, add the scallops and
sauté until they begin to turn opaque on the bottom, about 1 minute.
Sprinkle the scallops with the pepper and the remaining ¼ teaspoon salt
and turn them over. Continue to cook until opaque throughout and just
lightly browned but still soft and tender, about 45 seconds longer.

❀ Pour the remaining grapefruit juice over the scallops, reduce the heat
to low, and deglaze the pan, stirring with a wooden spoon to dislodge
any browned bits from the pan bottom. Using a slotted spatula, transfer
the scallops to the salad greens, arranging them on top and dividing
evenly. Drizzle the pan juices evenly over the tops.

❀ Garnish each plate with a tarragon sprig and serve immediately.

NUTRITIONAL ANALYSIS PER SERVING: Calories 170 (Kilojoules 714); Protein 15 g;
Carbohydrates 11 g; Total Fat 7 g; Saturated Fat 2 g; Cholesterol 36 mg; Sodium 577 mg;
Dietary Fiber 1 g

Fingerling Potato Salad with Shrimp and Baby Dill

PREP TIME: 15 MINUTES

COOKING TIME: 25 MINUTES,
   PLUS 6 HOURS FOR
   CHILLING

INGREDIENTS

2½ lb (1.25 kg) fingerling potatoes
   such as Ruby Crescent, Lady Finger,
   or Ratte (La Rote), unpeeled

1½ teaspoons salt

½ cup (4 oz/125 g) plain yogurt

½ cup (4 fl oz/125 ml) light sour
   cream

2 tablespoons mayonnaise

½ lb (250 g) cooked bay shrimp

¾ cup (2 oz/60 g) chopped green
   (spring) onion

½ cup (¾ oz/20 g) chopped baby dill,
   plus 1 or 2 sprigs for garnish

1 teaspoon ground pepper

Fingerling potatoes have the elongated, narrow shape of a finger. Some are only about 3 inches (7.5 cm) long, while others are 8–10 inches (20–25 cm). Generally thin-skinned with waxy, firm flesh, they are excellent boiling potatoes and, consequently, a fine choice for making potato salad. The tender leaves of baby dill are best for this delicate salad, although regular fresh dill can also be used.

SERVES 4

❀ In a large saucepan, combine the potatoes with water to cover by 2 inches (5 cm). Add 1 teaspoon of the salt and bring to a boil over high heat. Reduce the heat to medium and cook until the potatoes are tender when pierced with a sharp knife, 20–25 minutes.

❀ Drain the potatoes and, as soon as they are cool enough to handle, peel and cut crosswise into slices ¼ inch (6 mm) thick. Put the slices in a bowl and add the yogurt, sour cream, and mayonnaise. Turn gently to coat evenly. Add all but 4 of the shrimp, the green onion, chopped dill, pepper, and the remaining ½ teaspoon salt and turn again to mix well. Cover and refrigerate for at least 6 hours or up to 24 hours to allow the flavors to blend fully. Cover and refrigerate the reserved shrimp as well.

❀ To serve, top the salad with the reserved shrimp and a sprig or two of dill. Serve chilled.

NUTRITIONAL ANALYSIS PER SERVING: Calories 391 (Kilojoules 1,642); Protein 20 g; Carbohydrates 58 g; Total Fat 9 g; Saturated Fat 2 g; Cholesterol 126 mg; Sodium 846 mg; Dietary Fiber 5 g

Jerusalem Artichokes with Bacon and Balsamic Vinegar

PREP TIME: 15 MINUTES

COOKING TIME: 10 MINUTES

INGREDIENTS

1 lb (500 g) Jerusalem artichokes

2 or 3 slices Canadian bacon, about 2 oz (60 g) total weight, finely diced

1 tablespoon extra-virgin olive oil

3 tablespoons minced yellow onion

3 cloves roasted garlic, halved (optional)

½ teaspoon ground pepper

2 tablespoons balsamic vinegar

1 teaspoon water

COOKING TIP: Roasting garlic is easy and the cloves make a delicious addition to a number of dishes. Break a head of garlic apart into cloves and put them in a small baking dish. Drizzle the cloves with olive oil, and sprinkle with salt and pepper. Bake in a 400°F (200°C) oven until the cloves are tender, about 25 minutes. When cool enough to handle, peel off the paper skins.

Although Jerusalem artichokes have a nutty, potatolike flavor, they have a crisper texture than potatoes. They can be eaten raw or cooked and readily absorb other flavors, such as the salty taste of the Canadian bacon and the sweet tartness of the balsamic vinegar.

SERVES 4

❀ Using a vegetable peeler or paring knife, peel the Jerusalem artichokes. Then using a mandoline or sharp knife, cut into paper-thin slices. Set aside.

❀ In a frying pan over medium heat, cook the bacon, turning as needed, until crisp, about 5 minutes. Using a slotted spoon, transfer to paper towels to drain.

❀ If the bacon rendered any fat, pour off all but 1 teaspoon of the bacon fat from the pan. Add the olive oil to the pan and return to medium heat. When the oil is hot, add the Jerusalem artichokes, onion, roasted garlic, if using, and pepper. Sauté, stirring often, until the onion is translucent and the Jerusalem artichokes are tender to the bite but not soft, 4–5 minutes.

❀ Transfer the contents of the frying pan to a serving bowl, then return the pan to medium heat. Pour in the vinegar and water and deglaze the pan, stirring to dislodge any browned bits from the pan bottom. Add the contents of the pan to the bowl. Add the bacon and toss gently to mix. Serve immediately.

NUTRITIONAL ANALYSIS PER SERVING: Calories 116 (Kilojoules 487); Protein 5 g; Carbohydrates 15 g; Total Fat 4 g; Saturated Fat 1 g; Cholesterol 7 mg; Sodium 204 mg; Dietary Fiber 1 g

Fuyu Persimmon and Napa Cabbage Salad

PREP TIME: 15 MINUTES

INGREDIENTS

¼ cup (1 oz/30 g) sesame seeds

½ medium head napa cabbage, about 1 lb (500 g)

2 Fuyu persimmons

2 tablespoons corn or other light vegetable oil

2 tablespoons white wine vinegar or 1½ tablespoons lemon juice

½ teaspoon sugar

¼ teaspoon salt

¼ teaspoon ground pepper

As the weather grows cool, farmers' markets display the first sweet, tender heads of napa cabbage, sometimes called Chinese cabbage, and one of the season's special fruits, the persimmon. Be sure to choose the small, round Fuyu, which is sweet when still firm. The more elongated Hachiya develops its characteristic sugar-sweet flesh only when it is very soft and pulpy and is not suitable for slicing or serving when underripe.

SERVES 4

❋ In a small, dry frying pan over medium-low heat, toast the sesame seeds, stirring continuously, until lightly golden and fragrant, 2–3 minutes. Transfer to a small plate and set aside.

❋ Cut out the tough core from the base of the cabbage, then thinly slice the leaves. Place in a bowl. Trim away the stems from the persimmons, cut into quarters, and discard any seeds. Cut the persimmons into long, thin strips about ¼ inch (6 mm) wide. Add to the bowl holding the cabbage and toss to mix.

❋ In a small bowl, stir together the oil, vinegar or lemon juice, sugar, salt, and pepper. Pour over the cabbage-persimmon mixture and toss to coat well.

❋ Divide the salad evenly among individual plates or bowls. Sprinkle with the toasted sesame seeds and serve immediately.

NUTRITIONAL ANALYSIS PER SERVING: Calories 137 (Kilojoules 575); Protein 3 g; Carbohydrates 10 g; Total Fat 11 g; Saturated Fat 1 g; Cholesterol 0 mg; Sodium 153 mg; Dietary Fiber 2 g

Grilled Baby Leek, Green Garlic, and Roast Lamb Sandwich

PREP TIME: 15 MINUTES

COOKING TIME: 5 MINUTES,
    PLUS PREPARING FIRE

INGREDIENTS

8 baby leeks

8 stalks green garlic

¼ cup (2 fl oz/60 ml) extra-virgin
    olive oil

½ teaspoon salt

½ teaspoon ground pepper

½ cup (4 fl oz/125 ml) mayonnaise

2 cloves garlic, crushed and then
    minced

4 pieces rosemary or other herb-
    flavored focaccia, each about
    4 inches (10 cm) square

¾ lb (375 g) roast lamb, thinly sliced
    and warmed

4 butter (Boston) lettuce leaves

SERVING TIP: Baby leeks and green
garlic, cooked as described here, also
make a wonderful accompaniment
for freshly grilled lamb chops or
butterflied leg of lamb.

Among the treasures of spring and early summer are baby leeks and green garlic. The leeks are harvested when they are about the same width as a finger, and the garlic is pulled when it resembles a green onion, with the bulbous base barely formed. Their flavors are mild and delicate and particularly tasty when treated to brief grilling. If green garlic is unavailable, substitute one clove of regular garlic for each green garlic bulb.

SERVES 4

❀ Prepare a fire in a charcoal grill.

❀ Trim the leeks and the green garlic stalks to about 6 inches (15 cm) long, and slit them lengthwise about three-fourths of the way through. Lay them in a shallow baking dish and sprinkle with the olive oil and ¼ teaspoon each of the salt and pepper. Turn the leeks and green garlic in the oil to coat them well. Let stand for at least 15 minutes or for up to several hours before grilling.

❀ In a small bowl, stir together the mayonnaise, minced garlic, and the remaining ¼ teaspoon each salt and pepper until well mixed. Cover and refrigerate until needed.

❀ When the fire is ready, lay the leeks and green garlic on the grill rack. Grill until browned on the undersides, 2–3 minutes. Turn and continue to cook until golden and crisp at the edges, 1 minute or so longer. Transfer to a cutting board and chop; keep warm.

❀ Cut each focaccia square in half horizontally to make 2 pieces for each sandwich. Spread the cut side of each half with some of the mayonnaise. Sprinkle the bottom half of each square with one-fourth of the chopped leeks and garlic. Top with one-fourth of the sliced lamb and 1 lettuce leaf. Top with the other half of the focaccia square, mayonnaise side down. Cut the sandwiches on the diagonal and serve warm.

NUTRITIONAL ANALYSIS PER SERVING: Calories 809 (Kilojoules 3,398); Protein 34 g; Carbohydrates 53 g; Total Fat 53 g; Saturated Fat 12 g; Cholesterol 98 mg; Sodium 813 mg; Dietary Fiber 3 g

Red Cabbage and Apple Soup

PREP TIME: 20 MINUTES

COOKING TIME: 30 MINUTES

INGREDIENTS

1 head red cabbage, about ¾ lb (375 g)

4 Golden Delicious apples, about 1 lb (500 g) total weight

2 tablespoons unsalted butter

1 yellow onion, minced

¼ cup (2 fl oz/60 ml) red wine vinegar

4½ cups (36 fl oz/1.1 l) low-sodium beef broth

½ teaspoon salt

½ teaspoon ground pepper

2 teaspoons lemon juice

⅓ cup (3 fl oz/80 ml) light sour cream

¼ cup (⅓ oz/10 g) chopped fresh dill

This hearty and delicious soup gets an extra burst of flavor from the grated apple added just before serving. Golden Delicious apples are sweet and finely textured, but if you want a sharper-flavored, crisper variety, choose Granny Smith instead.

SERVES 4

❈ On a cutting board, using a large, sharp knife, cut the cabbage in half through the stem end. Cut out the tough core portions and discard. One at a time, place each half, cut side down, on the board and cut into very thin slices. Cut 2 of the unpeeled apples into quarters, core them, and then cut into 1-inch (2.5-cm) cubes. Set the cabbage and the cut-up apples aside separately.

❈ In a large saucepan over medium heat, melt the butter. When it is foaming, add the onion and sauté until translucent, 2–3 minutes. Add the apple cubes and sauté until softened slightly, another 3–4 minutes. Add the cabbage and sauté, stirring often, until it glistens and the color has lightened, 5–6 minutes. Add the vinegar and deglaze the pan, stirring to dislodge any browned bits from the pan bottom. Add the beef broth, salt, and pepper and bring to a boil over medium-high heat. Reduce the heat to low, cover, and simmer until tender, about 15 minutes.

❈ While the soup is simmering, peel, halve, and core the remaining 2 apples, then shred them finely. Place in a small bowl, add the lemon juice, and toss to coat. Set aside.

❈ When the soup is ready, remove from the heat and stir in three-fourths of the shredded apples. Ladle the soup into warmed bowls. Top each serving with a spoonful of the sour cream. Sprinkle the remaining grated apples and the dill over the top, dividing evenly. Serve at once.

NUTRITIONAL ANALYSIS PER SERVING: Calories 190 (Kilojoules 798); Protein 8 g; Carbohydrates 26 g; Total Fat 8 g; Saturated Fat 4 g; Cholesterol 22 mg; Sodium 412 mg; Dietary Fiber 4 g

Japanese Cucumbers with Soy-Sesame Dressing

PREP TIME: 20 MINUTES, PLUS
1 HOUR FOR MARINATING

INGREDIENTS

2 tablespoons sesame seeds

2 tablespoons unseasoned rice
    vinegar

1 tablespoon peanut oil

1 tablespoon soy sauce

½ teaspoon Asian sesame oil

2 Japanese cucumbers, each about
    8 inches (20 cm) long, sliced
    paper-thin on the diagonal

¼ cup (1¼ oz/37 g) minced red
    (Spanish) onion

2 tablespoons chopped fresh
    cilantro (fresh coriander)

PREP TIP: You can use a mandoline
to make the ultrathin slices of cucum-
ber called for here, or a sharp, thin-
bladed knife.

Japanese cucumbers are slender, long, and crisp and show only
bare evidence of seed development. Grown in greenhouses,
they are available most of the year and have a more intense
flavor than regular cucumbers. They do not need to be peeled,
although you can peel them if you prefer. Serve this salad to
precede or accompany a stir-fry dish or steamed or grilled fish.

SERVES 4

❀ In a small, dry frying pan over medium-low heat, toast the sesame
seeds, stirring continuously, until lightly golden and fragrant, 2–3 minutes. Transfer to a plate and set aside.

❀ In a bowl, combine the rice vinegar, peanut oil, soy sauce, and
sesame oil. Mix well with a fork. Add the cucumbers and onion, and
turn them in the sauce. Let stand at room temperature, turning from
time to time, for at least 1 hour to allow the flavors to blend. (Alternatively,
cover and refrigerate for up to 24 hours and serve chilled or at room
temperature.)

❀ To serve, sprinkle with the toasted sesame seeds and the cilantro.

NUTRITIONAL ANALYSIS PER SERVING: Calories 89 (Kilojoules 374); Protein 2 g;
Carbohydrates 7 g; Total Fat 6 g; Saturated Fat 1 g; Cholesterol 0 mg; Sodium 262 mg;
Dietary Fiber 2 g

Squash Flower and Black Olive Pasta

PREP TIME: 20 MINUTES

COOKING TIME: 10 MINUTES

INGREDIENTS

9 squash flowers

¾ lb (375 g) penne rigate, mostaccioli, or other dried short pasta

3 tablespoons extra-virgin olive oil

1 tablespoon unsalted butter

½ yellow onion, chopped

3 cloves garlic, minced

10 oz (315 g) oil-cured black olives, pitted and halved (about 2 cups)

2 teaspoons minced fresh thyme

1 teaspoon salt

1 teaspoon ground pepper

¼ cup (1 oz/30 g) grated Parmesan cheese

This brightly colored pasta can be made with the male or the female flowers of summer squashes or pumpkins. The male flowers are usually sold in bunches like bouquets, as they have long stems that can be put into water. The female blossoms, which have immature squashes attached, are sold by the piece. Should you choose the latter, you might like to thinly slice the tiny squashes and add them to the pasta.

SERVES 4

❀ Cut 8 of the squash flowers in half lengthwise. Remove and discard the furry anthers at their centers. Cut the flowers into long strips ¼ inch (6 mm) wide and set aside. Reserve the remaining flower for garnish.

❀ Bring a large pot three-fourths full of salted water to a boil. Add the pasta, stir well, and cook until al dente (tender but firm to the bite), about 8 minutes or according to the package directions.

❀ Meanwhile, in a frying pan over medium heat, warm 1 tablespoon of the olive oil with the butter. Add the onion and garlic and sauté until translucent, 3–4 minutes. Add the olives and 1 teaspoon of the thyme. Continue to sauté until the olives become plump, 3–4 minutes longer.

❀ Drain the pasta and place in a warmed serving bowl. Drizzle with the remaining 2 tablespoons olive oil, sprinkle with the salt and pepper, and toss to coat evenly. Add the olives and all their pan juices and toss to coat again. Finally, add the remaining 1 teaspoon thyme and the cut-up squash flowers and toss gently. Sprinkle with the cheese and garnish with the remaining whole squash flower. Serve immediately.

NUTRITIONAL ANALYSIS PER SERVING: Calories 721 (Kilojoules 3,024); Protein 16 g; Carbohydrates 73 g; Total Fat 43 g; Saturated Fat 8 g; Cholesterol 13 mg; Sodium 3,380 mg; Dietary Fiber 3 g

Pan-Seared Halibut with Sautéed Baby Vegetables

PREP TIME: 20 MINUTES

COOKING TIME: 10 MINUTES

INGREDIENTS

12 small, young turnips, with greens
intact

12 baby carrots

1 fennel bulb

1 tablespoon unsalted butter

1 teaspoon salt

½ teaspoon ground pepper

⅓ cup (3 fl oz/80 ml) dry white wine

4 halibut steaks or fillets, each about
5 oz (155 g) and ½ inch (12 mm)
thick

COOKING TIP: Other mild, firm-
fleshed white fish such as sea bass
or snapper may be substituted for
the halibut.

Baby turnips, carrots, and fennel are more mild in flavor and
more delicate in texture than when the vegetables are fully
mature. They cook a lot faster, too.

SERVES 4

❀ Trim the turnips, cutting off the green tops. Choose the nicest, smallest leaves and reserve them; discard the rest. Cut the turnips into slices
about ⅛ inch (3 mm) thick. Trim the carrots and cut in half lengthwise.
Cut off the stems, feathery tops, and bruised outer stalks from the fennel
bulb. Cut the bulb crosswise into slices about ⅛ inch (3 mm) thick.

❀ In a frying pan over medium-high heat, melt ½ tablespoon of the
butter. When it is foaming, add the turnips, fennel, and carrots and
sauté until softened, 2–3 minutes. Sprinkle with ½ teaspoon of the salt
and ¼ teaspoon of the pepper and continue to cook, stirring occasionally,
until lightly browned, 1–2 minutes longer. Add the turnip leaves to the
pan along with the white wine. Reduce the heat to low, cover, and cook
until the vegetables are tender, about 2 minutes longer. Keep warm.

❀ In a large frying pan over medium-high heat, melt the remaining
½ tablespoon butter. When it is foaming, add the fish, sprinkle with
the remaining ½ teaspoon salt and ¼ teaspoon pepper and cook until
browned on the underside, 1–2 minutes. Turn and continue to cook
until browned on the second side and opaque in the center, 2–3 minutes longer.

❀ To serve, spoon one-fourth of the vegetable mixture onto each warmed
individual plate. Place a piece of fish alongside, garnish with a turnip
leaf, and serve at once.

NUTRITIONAL ANALYSIS PER SERVING: Calories 275 (Kilojoules 1,155); Protein 27 g;
Carbohydrates 25 g; Total Fat 6 g; Saturated Fat 2 g; Cholesterol 45 mg; Sodium 854 mg;
Dietary Fiber 8 g

Grilled Pork Chops, Asian Pears, and Torpedo Onions

PREP TIME: 15 MINUTES

COOKING TIME: 20 MINUTES,
    PLUS PREPARING FIRE

INGREDIENTS

4 rib pork chops, each about 4 oz
    (125 g) and ¾ inch (2 cm) thick

4 tablespoons (¼ oz/7 g) fresh sage
    leaves

1 teaspoon salt

1 teaspoon ground pepper

3 Asian pears, peeled, halved, cored,
    and cut into wedges about ½ inch
    (12 mm) thick

2 red torpedo onions, cut into
    wedges about ½ inch (12 mm)
    thick

2 tablespoons canola or other light
    cooking oil

Asian pears, which come into farmers' markets in late summer and early autumn, are extremely sweet and very crisp. They make a fine accompaniment to sweet red onions, round or torpedo shaped, and pork chops. Cooked together on the grill, this combination picks up a smoky flavor. The same trio can also be cooked under the broiler (griller) or in a stovetop frying pan.

SERVES 4

❋ Prepare a fire in a charcoal grill.

❋ Sprinkle the pork chops with 2 tablespoons of the sage leaves and ½ teaspoon each of the salt and pepper. Set aside.

❋ In a bowl, mix together the pears and onions and drizzle with the oil. Toss to coat. Add the remaining ½ teaspoon each salt and pepper and 2 tablespoons sage. Stir to mix well. The onions will fall apart.

❋ When the fire is medium-hot, place an oiled grilling basket on the grill rack to preheat it. When it is hot, place the onions and pears in it, close the basket, and grill until golden on the underside, 4–5 minutes. Turn the basket and continue to cook until golden on the second side and tender when pierced, 4–5 minutes longer. Remove the onions and pears from the basket, transfer to a warmed platter, and keep warm.

❋ Place the pork chops on the grill rack and grill, turning once, until browned and the juices run clear when a chop is cut into with a knife, 3–4 minutes on each side.

❋ To serve, arrange the chops on the platter or warmed individual plates and spoon the pears and onions on top or alongside.

NUTRITIONAL ANALYSIS PER SERVING: Calories 344 (Kilojoules 1,445); Protein 14 g; Carbohydrates 28 g; Total Fat 21 g; Saturated Fat 5 g; Cholesterol 47 mg; Sodium 619 mg; Dietary Fiber 8 g

Terrine of Winter Kale and Yukon Gold Potatoes with Sausage

PREP TIME: 20 MINUTES

COOKING TIME: 1¼ HOURS

INGREDIENTS

1 clove garlic, lightly crushed

6½ tablespoons (3½ oz/105 g) unsalted butter

½ lb (250 g) spicy chicken sausages, casings removed

2–2½ lb (1–1.25 kg) Yukon gold or red or white new potatoes, unpeeled, thinly sliced

salt and ground pepper to taste

1 bunch kale, trimmed and coarsely chopped

2 oz (60 g) Monterey jack cheese, shredded

½ cup (4 fl oz/125 ml) milk

COOKING TIP: Don't be alarmed if the pan seems ready to overflow; the kale will wilt during baking.

The flavors here are similar to those of *caldo verde*, the famous Portuguese soup also made with kale, potatoes, and sausage. For a full meal, serve with Salad of Young Fennel, Parmesan, and Button Mushrooms (page 39) and something yummy for dessert.

SERVES 4–6

❂ Preheat an oven to 350°F (180°C). Rub the bottom and sides of a 2- to 2½-qt (2- to 2.5-l) rectangular baking dish with the garlic, then grease it with about ½ tablespoon of the butter.

❂ Crumble the sausage into a frying pan and cook over medium heat, stirring occasionally, until lightly browned, 5–7 minutes. Using a slotted spoon, transfer to paper towels to drain.

❂ Cut the remaining 6 tablespoons (3 oz/90 g) butter into bits. Make a layer of one-third of the potato slices, overlapping slightly, in the bottom and along the sides of the prepared baking dish. Dot with about one-fourth of the butter and sprinkle with salt and pepper. Top with one-third of the crumbled sausage, one-third of the kale, and one-third of the cheese. Repeat the layers twice, ending with a layer of cheese. Dot with the remaining butter, then pour the milk evenly over the top. Cover the dish tightly with aluminum foil.

❂ Bake until the potatoes are very tender when pierced with a knife, about 1 hour. Remove from the oven and let stand for about 10 minutes.

❂ To serve, run a knife along the sides of the terrine and invert it onto a cutting board. Cut into slices 1½–2 inches (4–5 cm) thick and transfer to warmed individual plates. Serve immediately.

NUTRITIONAL ANALYSIS PER SERVING: Calories 455 (Kilojoules 1,911); Protein 15 g; Carbohydrates 44 g; Total Fat 25 g; Saturated Fat 13 g; Cholesterol 95 mg; Sodium 325 mg; Dietary Fiber 7 g

Quesadillas with Heirloom Tomatoes and Sweet Corn Salsa

PREP TIME: 30 MINUTES

COOKING TIME: 20 MINUTES,
    PLUS PREPARING FIRE

INGREDIENTS

2 lb (1 kg) assorted heirloom or
    other tomatoes, coarsely chopped

1½ teaspoons salt

1 teaspoon ground pepper

4 ears of corn, white or yellow or
    a mixture, husks removed

2 tablespoons canola or other light
    vegetable oil

1 large, ripe avocado, halved, pitted,
    and peeled, and cut into ½-inch
    (12-mm) dice

½ cup (3 oz/90 g) minced red
    (Spanish) onion

¼ cup (⅓ oz/10 g) chopped fresh
    cilantro (fresh coriander)

1 or 2 serrano chiles, seeded and
    minced

2 cloves garlic, minced

2 tablespoons lime juice

½ teaspoon chili powder

8 flour tortillas, each about 10 inches
    (25 cm) in diameter

½ lb (250 g) Monterey jack or other
    mild cheese, shredded

COOKING TIP: To make a spicier
salsa, add 1 more serrano chile. For
a more mild version, omit the ser-
ranos entirely.

To make these quesadillas, use as many different heirloom tomato varieties as you can find, such as Black Krim, Green Grape, Marvel Stripe, and Mortgage Lifter. Of course, ordinary sun-ripened summer tomatoes will work fine as well. A salsa of grilled sweet corn spiked with chiles and cilantro provides the perfect finishing touch.

MAKES 8 QUESADILLAS; SERVES 4

✸ Prepare a fire in a charcoal grill.

✸ Place the chopped tomatoes in a bowl and add 1 teaspoon of the salt and ½ teaspoon of the pepper. Stir to mix and set aside.

✸ Brush the ears of corn with 1 tablespoon of the oil. When the coals are medium-hot, place the corn on the grill rack and grill, turning often, until tender and lightly bronzed, 8–10 minutes. Remove from the grill rack and let cool.

✸ In a bowl, combine the avocado, onion, cilantro, serrano chiles, garlic, lime juice, chili powder, and remaining ½ teaspoon each salt and pepper. Cut off the kernels from the corn cobs and add to the avocado mixture. Stir to mix well. Set aside.

✸ In a frying pan over medium-high heat, heat the remaining 1 table-spoon oil. When it is hot, place 1 tortilla in the pan and cook until the edges begin to curl slightly, 1–2 minutes. Sprinkle some cheese down the center. Using a spatula, fold the tortilla in half and press down on the top. Cook until the underside is golden brown, about 30 seconds, then turn and continue to cook on the second side until golden brown and the cheese has melted, about 30 seconds longer. Remove from the pan and keep warm. Repeat until all the tortillas are cooked.

✸ Spoon several tablespoons of the tomatoes and the corn salsa inside each quesadilla and serve at once.

NUTRITIONAL ANALYSIS PER SERVING: Calories 918 (Kilojoules 3,856); Protein 32 g; Carbohydrates 108 g; Total Fat 44 g; Saturated Fat 14 g; Cholesterol 60 mg; Sodium 1,759 mg; Dietary Fiber 13 g

Sautéed Chicken Breasts with Champagne Grapes

PREP TIME: 15 MINUTES

COOKING TIME: 15 MINUTES

INGREDIENTS

4 boneless, skinless chicken breast
halves, about 6 oz (185 g) each

2 teaspoons unsalted butter

1 cup (6 oz/185 g) champagne
grapes, plus 4 small clusters for
garnish (optional)

¼ cup (2 fl oz/60 ml) dry white wine

¼ cup (2 fl oz/60 ml) chicken broth

3 tablespoons minced fresh cilantro
(fresh coriander)

¼ teaspoon ground pepper

Champagne grapes, also known as Zante, are the tiny grapes that become currants when dried. Ready for picking in autumn, they grow in tightly formed clusters that can be added whole to dishes or separated into singular grapes, as you like. If you can't find champagne grapes at your farmers' market, instead use a variety of different-colored grapes, seeding them first if necessary. Serve the chicken and grapes with steamed spinach and garlic mashed potatoes.

SERVES 4

❀ Rinse the chicken breasts and pat dry with paper towels. In a non-stick frying pan over medium-high heat, melt the butter. When it foams, add the chicken breasts and sear, turning once, until lightly browned, 30–60 seconds on each side. Add 1 tablespoon of the grapes, stir for a few seconds, then add the wine and broth and deglaze the pan, stirring and scraping to dislodge any browned bits from the pan bottom. Reduce the heat to low, cover tightly, and simmer just until the chicken is opaque throughout, 7–8 minutes.

❀ Add the remaining measured grapes and all but 1 teaspoon of the cilantro. Stir well, cover, and cook just long enough to warm the grapes through, 30–60 seconds. Season with the pepper.

❀ Transfer the chicken breasts to warmed individual plates. Pour one-fourth of the pan juices and grapes over each portion. Garnish with the remaining 1 teaspoon cilantro and, if you like, the grape clusters.

NUTRITIONAL ANALYSIS PER SERVING: Calories 257 (Kilojoules 1,079); Protein 40 g; Carbohydrates 10 g; Total Fat 4 g; Saturated Fat 2 g; Cholesterol 104 mg; Sodium 175 mg; Dietary Fiber 1 g

Penne with Sautéed Radicchio, Fennel, and Prosciutto

PREP TIME: 15 MINUTES

COOKING TIME: 20 MINUTES

INGREDIENTS

2 heads Treviso or regular radicchio, about 1 lb (500 g) total weight

1 fennel bulb

2 tablespoons unsalted butter

2 tablespoons plus 1 teaspoon olive oil

3 cloves garlic, chopped

1 teaspoon salt

1 teaspoon ground pepper

¾ lb (375 g) penne

¼ lb (125 g) prosciutto or Virginia ham, cut into long, narrow strips

1 tablespoon minced fresh thyme

shaved or grated Parmesan cheese (optional)

COOKING TIP: Other bite-sized pasta shapes such as farfalle, fusilli, or mostaccioli may be substituted for the penne.

An Italian winter favorite, Treviso radicchio is an elongated variety with thick, white midribs and pale red to burgundy leaves. Like other radicchio, it turns brown when cooked, but has an extraordinary flavor. Here, it is sautéed with another popular Italian vegetable, pale green fennel, which tastes mildly of licorice. Serve this hearty pasta dish with a romaine (cos) salad dotted with Gorgonzola cheese.

SERVES 4–6

❁ Trim away the tough stem, then cut each radicchio head lengthwise into pieces ½ inch (12 mm) wide. Cut off the stems, feathery tops, and bruised outer stalks from the fennel bulb. Then cut lengthwise into julienne strips ¼ inch (6 mm) thick.

❁ In a frying pan over medium-high heat, melt the butter with 2 tablespoons of the olive oil. When the butter foams, add the garlic and sauté until translucent, 2–3 minutes. Add the radicchio and fennel and ½ teaspoon each of the salt and pepper. Reduce the heat to low and sauté, stirring often, until the fennel is translucent and tender and the radicchio is lightly browned, about 10 minutes.

❁ Meanwhile, bring a large pot three-fourths full of salted water to a boil. Add the pasta, stir well, and cook until al dente (tender but firm to the bite), about 8 minutes or according to the package directions.

❁ Drain the pasta and transfer to a warmed serving bowl. Add the radicchio-fennel mixture and toss to coat evenly.

❁ In the same frying pan over medium heat, warm the 1 teaspoon olive oil. Add the prosciutto or Virginia ham and sauté just long enough to heat through, 1–2 minutes. Add to the pasta and toss to distribute evenly. Add the remaining ½ teaspoon each salt and pepper and the thyme. Toss again, put the cheese on top, if desired, and serve immediately.

NUTRITIONAL ANALYSIS PER SERVING: Calories 434 (Kilojoules 1,823); Protein 17 g; Carbohydrates 57 g; Total Fat 15 g; Saturated Fat 5 g; Cholesterol 31 mg; Sodium 1,189 mg; Dietary Fiber 3 g

Pork and Nopales Stew with Purslane and Cilantro

PREP TIME: 30 MINUTES

COOKING TIME: 3¼ HOURS

INGREDIENTS

2 lb (1 kg) lean pork butt or shoulder,
  cut into 2-inch (5-cm) cubes

2 teaspoons salt

4–6 pasilla chiles

1½–2 cups (12–16 fl oz/375–500 ml)
  boiling water

3 jalapeño chiles, seeded and
  chopped

1 large yellow onion, chopped

4 cloves garlic, chopped

1 piece fresh ginger, about 2 inches
  (5 cm), peeled and chopped

1 teaspoon ground pepper

1½ lb (750 g) tomatoes, peeled,
  seeded, and chopped

2 cups (16 fl oz/500 ml) chicken
  broth

1 large nopal cactus pad

1 cup (1 oz/30 g) fresh purslane
  leaves

¼ cup (¼ oz/7 g) fresh cilantro
  (fresh coriander) leaves

PREP TIP: Choose nopales that are
bright green, indicating they are
young and tender and harvested
from the plant's new growth. They
should also be firm and neither
wrinkled nor showing signs of mold.

Nopales, or cactus pads, have a delightful citruslike flavor and a
smooth texture. Purslane also has a slight citrus flavor. If you
cannot find purslane, omit it, as there is no good substitute.

SERVES 6

❁ In a heavy-bottomed saucepan, combine the pork with water to cover
by 2 inches (5 cm). Add 1 teaspoon of the salt and bring to a boil over
high heat. Reduce the heat to low, cover, and simmer until the pork is
tender, 1½–2 hours.

❁ Meanwhile, place a frying pan over medium-high heat. Place the
pasilla chiles in the pan and toast, turning once, until fragrant and lightly
browned, about 1 minute on each side. Transfer to a heatproof bowl and
pour in enough boiling water to cover fully. Let stand for 30 minutes.
Remove from the water (reserve the soaking water), discard the skins
and seeds, and coarsely chop the chiles.

❁ In a blender or food processor, combine the pasillas, jalapeños,
onion, garlic, ginger, pepper, and 3 or 4 tablespoons of the reserved
soaking water. Purée until a medium-thick paste forms, adding more
water if necessary to achieve the correct consistency. Set aside.

❁ When the pork is ready, drain it and place in a clean saucepan. Add
the chile mixture, tomatoes, and chicken broth. Bring to a boil over high
heat, reduce the heat to low, and simmer, uncovered, until tender
enough to cut with a fork, about 45 minutes.

❁ If the thorns have not been removed from the cactus pad, hold it with
tongs and scrape away the thorns with a sharp knife. Peel off the skin,
starting at the outer edges. Cut the pad into ½-inch (12-mm) squares.
(The stew can be made ahead to this point. Cover and refrigerate for
up to 24 hours.)

❁ Add the cactus and purslane to the pork and cook until tender and
easily pierced with a knife, 20–30 minutes longer. Much of the liquid
will be gone, leaving a thick sauce.

❁ Garnish with the cilantro and serve at once.

NUTRITIONAL ANALYSIS PER SERVING: Calories 300 (Kilojoules 1,260); Protein 32 g;
Carbohydrates 12 g; Total Fat 13 g; Saturated Fat 4 g; Cholesterol 103 mg; Sodium 1,231 mg;
Dietary Fiber 3 g

Stir-fried Eggplant and Tofu with Garlic and Chiles

PREP TIME: 20 MINUTES

COOKING TIME: 20 MINUTES

INGREDIENTS

2 tablespoons sesame seeds

2 tablespoons soy sauce

2 tablespoons dry white wine,
  dry sherry, or unseasoned rice
  vinegar

1 teaspoon cornstarch (cornflour)

6 tablespoons (3 fl oz/90 ml) corn
  or other light vegetable oil

4 cloves garlic, minced

4 serrano chiles, seeded and minced

2 red Anaheim chiles, seeded and
  cut into 1-inch (2.5-cm) squares

3 or 4 Asian (slender) eggplants
  (aubergines), about 1 lb (500 g)
  total weight, cut into 1-inch
  (2.5-cm) cubes

1 lb (500 g) firm tofu, drained and
  cut into 1-inch (2.5-cm) cubes

¼ cup (⅓ oz/10 g) chopped fresh
  cilantro (fresh coriander)

This is a quick and easy way to enjoy two of the most colorful vegetables of summer and autumn, eggplants and chiles. The Asian eggplant has a thinner skin and more delicate flesh than the globe eggplant and generally has fewer seeds as well, making it a good candidate for quick cooking. Serve with steamed white rice.

SERVES 4

❀ In a small, dry frying pan over medium-low heat, toast the sesame seeds, stirring continuously, until lightly golden and fragrant, 2–3 minutes. Transfer to a small plate and set aside.

❀ In a small bowl, stir together the soy sauce; wine, sherry, or vinegar; and cornstarch until the cornstarch dissolves. Set aside.

❀ In a wok or large, deep frying pan over high heat, heat 2 tablespoons of the oil. When the oil is hot, add the garlic and serrano chiles and toss and stir until fragrant, about 30 seconds. Add 2 more tablespoons of the oil and, when hot, add the Anaheim chiles. Toss and stir for another 30 seconds. Add the remaining 2 tablespoons oil and again allow to heat. Then add the eggplant and cook, turning often, until the eggplant has softened and browned a bit, 10–12 minutes.

❀ Quickly stir the soy mixture and then add to the pan along with the tofu. Toss and stir to coat all the ingredients, then cover and cook until the eggplant is tender, the tofu is heated through, and the liquid has thickened slightly, 1–2 minutes longer.

❀ Remove from the heat and stir in the cilantro. Transfer to a warmed serving dish and sprinkle with the sesame seeds. Serve immediately.

NUTRITIONAL ANALYSIS PER SERVING: Calories 425 (Kilojoules 1,785); Protein 21 g; Carbohydrates 17 g; Total Fat 33 g; Saturated Fat 4 g; Cholesterol 0 mg; Sodium 538 mg; Dietary Fiber 3 g

Spicy Black Bean Beef with Thai Basil and Jasmine Rice

PREP TIME: 25 MINUTES,
PLUS 30 MINUTES FOR
MARINATING BEEF

COOKING TIME: 5 MINUTES

INGREDIENTS

FOR THE BLACK BEAN SAUCE

2 tablespoons fermented black beans

4 cloves garlic, minced

1 piece fresh ginger, 1½ inches
   (4 cm), peeled and minced

2 tablespoons dry sherry or dry
   white wine

1 teaspoon soy sauce

2 teaspoons soy sauce

1 teaspoon dry sherry or dry white
   wine

2 teaspoons cornstarch (cornflour)

½ teaspoon sugar

1¼ teaspoons salt

1 lb (500 g) beef top sirloin, about
   1 inch (2.5 cm) thick, sliced
   paper-thin across the grain

3 tablespoons peanut oil

2 cups (16 fl oz/500 ml) water

1 cup (7 oz/220 g) jasmine rice

¼ cup (⅓ oz/10 g) chopped or
   snipped fresh Thai basil

Thai or holy basil, which begins to appear in farmers' markets in late spring and early summer, has distinctive deep purple stems, dark green leaves, and lavender blossoms. Its aniselike flavor is more perfumed and less tart than that of Italian basil and is best enjoyed raw. (If unavailable, substitute purple or Italian basil.) If you like, stir in 1-inch (2.5-cm) pieces of cooked asparagus or broccoli florets just before serving.

SERVES 3 OR 4

✻ To make the black bean sauce, in a small bowl, stir together the black beans, garlic, ginger, sherry or white wine, and soy sauce. Set aside.

✻ In a bowl large enough to hold the beef, combine the 2 teaspoons soy sauce, 1 teaspoon sherry or white wine, cornstarch, sugar, and ¼ teaspoon of the salt. Stir until well mixed, then add the beef and stir to coat evenly. Pour 1 tablespoon of the peanut oil over the beef and marinate at room temperature for 30 minutes.

✻ While the beef is marinating, cook the rice. In a heavy saucepan over medium-high heat, bring the water to a boil. Add the remaining 1 teaspoon salt and the rice. When the water returns to a boil, reduce the heat to low, cover, and cook until the rice is tender and the water has been fully absorbed, about 20 minutes.

✻ About 5 minutes before the rice is ready, in a wok or large, deep frying pan over high heat, heat the remaining 2 tablespoons oil. When the oil is very hot, add the beef and its marinade and toss and stir until the meat has changed color but is still pink, 2–3 minutes. Pour in the black bean mixture and continue to toss and stir just until the meat is barely cooked through, 1–2 minutes longer. Stir in half of the basil.

✻ To serve, mound the rice in a serving bowl or divide evenly among individual bowls or plates and top with the beef. Garnish with the remaining basil.

NUTRITIONAL ANALYSIS PER SERVING: Calories 536 (Kilojoules 2,251); Protein 26 g; Carbohydrates 42 g; Total Fat 28 g; Saturated Fat 9 g; Cholesterol 76 mg; Sodium 1,263 mg; Dietary Fiber 0 g

Roast Chicken Stuffed with Winter Savory and Preserved Lemons

PREP TIME: 25 MINUTES, PLUS
2 MONTHS FOR CURING
LEMONS

COOKING TIME: 1¼ HOURS

INGREDIENTS

FOR THE PRESERVED LEMONS
4½ qt (4½ l) water

7–10 firm lemons

⅔ cup (5 oz/155 g) sea salt

2 cinnamon sticks

4 teaspoons coriander seeds

2 teaspoons peppercorns

8 whole cloves

1 cup (8 fl oz/250 ml) olive oil, plus
more if needed

1 chicken, 2½–3 lb (1.25–1.5 kg)

3 or 4 preserved lemons, quartered
lengthwise, plus more for garnish
(optional)

1 teaspoon salt

1 teaspoon ground pepper

1 tablespoon fresh winter savory
leaves; 4 or 5 sprigs, each
about 4 inches (10 cm) long; plus
more for garnish (optional)

PREP TIP: You need first to allow
some 2 months for the preserved
lemons to absorb the flavor of the
spices and brine. Or you can purchase this Moroccan flavoring ready-
made at some specialty food stores.
Once opened, keep in the refrigerator
for up to 3 months.

Preserved citrus fruits deliver a complexity of tastes to roast
chicken, meat and poultry stews, and grains.

SERVES 4

❈ To preserve the lemons, pour 3 qt (3 l) of the water into a nonaluminum saucepan and bring to a boil. When the water is boiling, add the
lemons and return to a boil. Cook the lemons until softened, 3–4 minutes. Drain and immerse in cold water until cool enough to handle. Cut
a shallow X in the bottom of each lemon.

❈ In the same saucepan, combine the remaining 6 cups (48 fl oz/1.5 l)
water, the salt, cinnamon sticks, coriander seeds, peppercorns, and
cloves to make a brine. Bring to a boil. Remove from the heat.

❈ Sterilize 2 wide-mouthed glass canning jars, each large enough to
hold 4 or 5 lemons.

❈ Tightly pack the whole lemons into the hot, dry sterilized jars. Pour
in the 1 cup (8 fl oz/250 ml) olive oil, dividing it evenly if necessary,
then pour in the hot brine, filling to within ½ inch (12 mm) of the
rim(s). If there is not enough brine, use olive oil. Tap the jars on the
work surface to remove any air bubbles. Seal the jars tightly. Store in
a cool, dark place for at least 2 months or up to 6 months.

❈ Preheat an oven to 350°F (180°C).

❈ Rinse the chicken and pat dry with paper towels. Rub the surface of
the chicken with a preserved lemon quarter, then rub with the salt, pepper, and the winter savory leaves. Stuff 4 or 5 winter savory sprigs and
all but 3 of the remaining lemon quarters into the cavity of the chicken.
Truss the chicken, if you like, and put it in a roasting pan.

❈ Roast until an instant-read thermometer inserted into the thickest
part of the thigh not touching the bone registers 165°–170°F (74°–77°C),
or until the juices run clear when a thigh joint is pierced, about 1¼ hours.

❈ Remove the chicken from the oven, cover loosely with aluminum foil,
and let stand for 10 minutes. Garnish with preserved lemons and sprigs
of winter savory, if you like. Carve into pieces and serve.

NUTRITIONAL ANALYSIS PER SERVING: Calories 451 (Kilojoules 1,894); Protein 40 g;
Carbohydrates 11 g; Total Fat 30 g; Saturated Fat 7 g; Cholesterol 123 mg; Sodium 1,186 mg;
Dietary Fiber 0 g

Braised Duck Thighs with Fresh Plums

PREP TIME: 15 MINUTES

COOKING TIME: 25 MINUTES

INGREDIENTS

1 teaspoon salt

4 skinless duck thighs

1 teaspoon ground pepper

¼ cup (2 fl oz/60 ml) brandy

8 prune plums, halved and pitted, or 4 round, purple-skinned, amber-fleshed plums, quartered

1 teaspoon sugar

4–5 tablespoons (2–2½ fl oz/ 60–75 ml) chicken broth

Smallish oval, amber-fleshed prune plums, also known as Italian, French, or sugar plums, are a seasonal specialty of late summer and early autumn. Their intense sweetness pairs splendidly with the robust flavor of duck. Larger, round, amber-fleshed varieties can be substituted. Serve with spaetzle and garlic-sautéed chard, or with rice pilaf and steamed broccoli drizzled with lemon juice.

SERVES 4

❀ Sprinkle the salt in a nonstick frying pan just large enough to hold the 4 duck thighs. Place the pan over high heat. When the pan is hot, place the thighs in it and sprinkle them with the pepper. Sear, turning once, until browned, 1–2 minutes on each side. Pour in the brandy and add half of the plums. Reduce the heat to medium-high and deglaze the pan, stirring to dislodge any browned bits from the pan bottom, 1–2 minutes.

❀ In a small bowl, dissolve the sugar in 4 tablespoons (2 fl oz/60 ml) chicken broth and pour into the pan. Reduce the heat to low and cover tightly. Cook for 7–8 minutes. Uncover and check to see if the pan has dried out. If it has, add another 1 tablespoon broth. Turn over the duck, cover the pan, and continue to cook until the duck is cooked through and tender, 7–8 minutes longer. Transfer the duck pieces to a plate.

❀ Skim or pour off any fat from the pan. There should be about 2 tablespoons of juices remaining in the pan. Return the pan to medium-low heat and return the thighs and any collected juices on the plate to the pan along with the remaining plums. Cook, turning the thighs once, until the just-added plums are heated through, 2–3 minutes.

❀ To serve, transfer the duck thighs to warmed individual plates and spoon some of the sauce and plums over them. Serve immediately.

NUTRITIONAL ANALYSIS PER SERVING: Calories 296 (Kilojoules 1,243); Protein 38 g; Carbohydrates 16 g; Total Fat 8 g; Saturated Fat 2 g; Cholesterol 134 mg; Sodium 791 mg; Dietary Fiber 2 g

Linguine with Roasted Late-Summer Tomato Sauce

PREP TIME: 15 MINUTES

COOKING TIME: 1¾ HOURS

INGREDIENTS

2 lb (1 kg) very ripe tomatoes

¾ lb (375 g) dried linguine

chopped fresh basil (optional)

grated Parmesan cheese (optional)

COOKING TIP: Highly acidic tomatoes will result in a tart sauce. Taste the puréed sauce and, if necessary, add a pinch or two of sugar to balance the flavor.

Slow cooking concentrates the flavor of late-summer tomatoes so that no other seasonings, not even salt, are needed in this sauce. Once the tomatoes are cooked down to a thick, jamlike consistency, they are put through a food mill to remove skin and seeds, with a smooth sauce the result. You may, however, peel and seed the tomatoes first, roast them, and forgo the food mill, producing a chunkier sauce.

SERVES 4

❀ Preheat an oven to 350°F (180°C).

❀ Cut out the core from each tomato but leave the tomatoes whole. Place them in a shallow roasting pan and roast until soft, about 45 minutes. Remove from the oven and, using a fork, smash each tomato, releasing the pulp and juices from the skin. Return the pan to the oven and continue to roast, stirring and scraping the edges of the pan occasionally, until the tomatoes are thick and jamlike, about 1 hour longer. Remove from the oven and pass through a food mill or coarse sieve placed over a small bowl. You should have about ¾ cup (6 fl oz/180 ml) thick sauce.

❀ About 15 minutes before the sauce is ready, bring a large pot three-fourths full of salted water to a boil. Add the pasta, stir well, and cook until al dente (tender but firm to the bite), about 8 minutes or according to package directions.

❀ Drain the pasta and return to the pot. Add all but 2–3 tablespoons of the sauce. Toss well, coating the pasta evenly with the sauce. Divide among 4 warmed individual bowls. Drizzle the top of each bowl with the remaining sauce. If desired, sprinkle with basil and Parmesan cheese.

NUTRITIONAL ANALYSIS PER SERVING: Calories 359 (Kilojoules 1,508); Protein 13 g; Carbohydrates 73 g; Total Fat 2 g; Saturated Fat 0 g; Cholesterol 0 mg; Sodium 315 mg; Dietary Fiber 5 g

Hachiya Persimmon Bar Cookies with Lemon Icing

PREP TIME: 30 MINUTES

COOKING TIME: 25 MINUTES,
    PLUS 1 HOUR FOR COOLING

INGREDIENTS

2 or 3 very ripe, very soft Hachiya
    persimmons

1½ teaspoons lemon juice

1 teaspoon baking soda (bicarbonate
    of soda)

1 egg

1 cup (8 fl oz/250 ml) canola or
    other light vegetable oil

½ lb (250 g) pitted dates, finely
    chopped

1¾ cups (9 oz/280 g) all-purpose
    (plain) flour

1 teaspoon salt

1 teaspoon ground cinnamon

1 teaspoon ground nutmeg

¼ teaspoon ground cloves

1 cup (4 oz/125 g) chopped walnuts

FOR THE LEMON ICING

1 cup (4 oz/125 g) confectioners'
    (icing) sugar

2 tablespoons lemon juice

The thick pulp of the Hachiya persimmon gives a moist and tender texture and wonderful sweetness to this autumn spice cookie. Be sure to use the dark orange, pointed Hachiya, as the firm-fleshed Fuyu persimmon doesn't produce the soft pulp necessary for these cookies.

MAKES ABOUT 2½ DOZEN BAR COOKIES

❀ Preheat an oven to 350°F (180°C). Butter and flour a 10-by-15-inch (25-by-38-cm) jelly-roll (Swiss roll) pan.

❀ Peel 2 of the persimmons and remove any seeds and discard. Measure the pulp; you need 1 cup (8 fl oz/250 ml). Peel and seed the third persimmon if needed to reach the desired volume. Place the pulp in a bowl and add the lemon juice and baking soda; set aside.

❀ In a large bowl, lightly beat the egg until blended. Add the oil and dates and stir to mix well. In another bowl, stir together the flour, salt, cinnamon, nutmeg, and cloves. Dividing the flour mixture into 3 batches, whisk the flour mixture into the egg mixture alternately with the pulp, beginning and ending with the flour mixture. Stir in the nuts. Pour into the prepared pan.

❀ Bake until a knife inserted into the center comes out clean, about 25 minutes. Transfer to a rack and let cool for 5 minutes.

❀ Meanwhile, make the lemon icing: In a bowl, combine the confectioners' sugar and the lemon juice. Stir until smooth.

❀ Spread with the glaze, then let cool thoroughly, about 1 hour. Cut into bars 3 inches (7.5 cm) long by 1½ inches (4 cm) wide. To store, place between layers of waxed paper in an airtight container. Refrigerate for up to 1 week.

NUTRITIONAL ANALYSIS PER BAR COOKIE: Calories 163 (Kilojoules 685); Protein 2 g; Carbohydrates 18 g; Total Fat 10 g; Saturated Fat 1 g; Cholesterol 7 mg; Sodium 124 mg; Dietary Fiber 1 g

Tarte Tatin of Winter Pears

SERVES 6–8

PREP TIME: 30 MINUTES,
   PLUS 15 MINUTES FOR
   CHILLING DOUGH

COOKING TIME: 1 HOUR

INGREDIENTS

FOR THE PASTRY DOUGH

2 cups (10 oz/315 g) all-purpose
   (plain) flour

½ teaspoon salt

½ cup (4 oz/125 g) plus 1 tablespoon
   chilled unsalted butter

6 tablespoons (3 fl oz/90 ml) ice
   water

3 tablespoons unsalted butter

¼ cup (2 oz/60 g) granulated sugar

3 or 4 firm, ripe winter Nellis or
   Bosc pears (about 2 lb/1 kg total
   weight), peeled, halved, and cored

½ cup (4 oz/120 g) firmly packed
   brown sugar

2 tablespoons finely chopped
   crystallized ginger

1 tablespoon lemon juice

½ teaspoon ground mace

¼ teaspoon ground cinnamon

¼ teaspoon ground cloves

PREP TIP: Apples may be substituted
for the pears to make a traditional
version of tarte Tatin.

❋ To make the pastry dough, in a bowl, stir together the flour and salt. Cut the butter into ½-inch (12-mm) chunks and add to the flour mixture. Using a pastry blender or 2 knives, cut in the butter until pea-sized pieces form. Add the ice water 1 tablespoon at a time, stirring lightly with a fork and then rubbing with your fingertips. Gather the dough into a ball, wrap it in plastic wrap, and refrigerate for 15 minutes.

❋ Preheat an oven to 375°F (190°C). Using 1 tablespoon of the butter, grease a 12-inch (30-cm) round baking dish with 2-inch (5-cm) sides, preferably of glass so you can watch the syrup forming. Sprinkle the sugar evenly over the dish bottom.

❋ Place the pears, cut sides up, in a tightly packed layer in the prepared baking dish. If necessary, slice a half lengthwise and use the slices to fill in any gaps between the halves. Sprinkle ¼ cup (2 oz/60 g) of the brown sugar over the pears. Top with the crystallized ginger and the lemon juice. Cut the remaining 2 tablespoons butter into bits and dot the tops of the pears. Stir together the remaining ¼ cup (2 oz/60 g) brown sugar and the mace, cinnamon, and cloves. Sprinkle the mixture evenly over the pears.

❋ On a floured work surface, roll out the dough a little larger than the diameter of the baking dish and a scant ¼ inch (6 mm) thick. Drape the pastry over the rolling pin and transfer it to the baking dish. Carefully undrape the pastry over the pears. Tuck the edges of the pastry down to the bottom of the dish to form an interior rim that will encircle the pears once the tart is turned out of the dish. Prick the top all over with a fork.

❋ Bake until the crust is golden brown, the pears are tender, and a thickened, golden syrup has formed in the dish, about 1 hour.

❋ Remove from the oven and let stand for 5 minutes. To unmold, run a knife around the inside edge of the baking dish to loosen the sides of the tart. Invert a platter on top of the baking dish and, using pot holders to hold the platter and the baking dish tightly together, flip them. Lift off the baking dish, gently removing any of the pears that may have stuck to the dish and repositioning them on the tart. Serve warm.

NUTRITIONAL ANALYSIS PER SERVING: Calories 483 (Kilojoules 2,029); Protein 5 g; Carbohydrates 76 g; Total Fat 19 g; Saturated Fat 11 g; Cholesterol 49 mg; Sodium 179 mg; Dietary Fiber 4 g

Meyer Lemon Tartlets

MAKES 16 TARTLETS

PREP TIME: 20 MINUTES,
PLUS 15 MINUTES FOR
CHILLING DOUGH

COOKING TIME: 30 MINUTES

INGREDIENTS

FOR THE PASTRY DOUGH

2 cups (10 oz/315 g) all-purpose (plain) flour

½ teaspoon salt

½ cup (4 oz/125 g) plus 1 tablespoon chilled unsalted butter

6 tablespoons (3 fl oz/90 ml) ice water

FOR THE LEMON FILLING

1¼ cups (10 oz/315 g) sugar

⅓ cup (1½ oz/45 g) cornstarch (cornflour)

¼ teaspoon salt

1½ cups (12 fl oz/375 ml) boiling water

3 egg yolks

⅓ cup (3 fl oz/80 ml) Meyer lemon juice

2 tablespoons unsalted butter

2 teaspoons grated lemon zest

COOKING TIP: The juice of the thin-skinned Meyer lemon is wonderfully sweet, and the zest is very aromatic. If you can't locate Meyer lemons, add 1 teaspoon sugar to ⅓ cup (3 fl oz/80 ml) regular lemon juice.

❀ To make the pastry dough, in a bowl, stir together the flour and salt. Cut the butter into ½-inch (12-mm) chunks and add to the flour mixture. Using a pastry blender or 2 knives, cut in the butter until pea-sized pieces form. Add the ice water 1 tablespoon at a time, stirring lightly with a fork and then rubbing with your fingertips. Gather the dough into a ball, wrap it in plastic wrap, and refrigerate for 15 minutes.

❀ Preheat an oven to 425°F (220°C). Have ready sixteen 2-inch (5-cm) fluted tartlet pans with removable bottoms.

❀ On a floured work surface, roll out the dough ¼ inch (6 mm) thick. Using a 2½- to 3-inch (6- to 7-cm) round biscuit cutter, cut out 16 rounds. Press each round into the bottom and sides of a tartlet pan. Place the pans on a baking sheet. Line them with aluminum foil and partially fill with pie weights.

❀ Bake until lightly golden, 12–15 minutes. Remove from the oven and remove the weights and foil. Prick any bubbles with a fork and return to the oven. Continue to bake until golden, about 5 minutes longer. Remove from the oven and let cool. Reduce the oven temperature to 350°F (180°C).

❀ Meanwhile, make the filling: In the top pan of a double boiler, combine the sugar, cornstarch, and salt. Add the 1½ cups (12 fl oz/375 ml) boiling water and whisk until well mixed. Place the pan directly over medium-low heat and cook, stirring constantly with a wooden spoon, until the mixture thickens and becomes a clearer yellow, about 10 minutes.

❀ Pour the egg yolks into a bowl, stir briefly to blend, then whisk in about ¼ cup (2 fl oz/60 ml) of the hot cornstarch mixture. Pour the egg yolks into the cornstarch mixture, stirring constantly. Set the top pan over (but not touching) boiling water in the bottom pan and cook, stirring constantly, until beginning to thicken, about 2 minutes longer. Remove from the heat and stir in the lemon juice, butter, and lemon zest. Let cool for 5–10 minutes. Spoon the filling into the pastry shells.

❀ Bake until set and the surfaces are glazed, about 10 minutes. Let cool on racks for 10 minutes. Remove from the pans and serve warm.

NUTRITIONAL ANALYSIS PER TARTLET: Calories 219 (Kilojoules 920); Protein 2 g; Carbohydrates 34 g; Total Fat 8 g; Saturated Fat 5 g; Cholesterol 59 mg; Sodium 112 mg; Dietary Fiber 0 g

Satsuma Mandarin and Star Anise Compote

PREP TIME: 15 MINUTES

COOKING TIME: 1¼ HOURS,
    PLUS 1 HOUR STANDING
    TIME

INGREDIENTS

1 cup (8 fl oz/250 ml) water

1 cup (8 oz/250 g) sugar

4 whole star anise

1 tablespoon grated orange zest

6 satsuma mandarins

MAKE-AHEAD TIP: The dish can be fully assembled, covered, and refrigerated for up to 24 hours before serving. It can then be served chilled or at room temperature.

The sweet, seedless satsuma, one of the many varieties of mandarin orange, is among the earliest of winter citrus to arrive at farmers' markets. This simple dessert shows off the satsuma's sparkling flavor and includes the slightly exotic touch of star anise. Any mandarin orange may be used in place of the satsuma.

SERVES 4

❁ In a saucepan over medium heat, combine the water and sugar. Heat, stirring often, until the sugar dissolves and a thin syrup forms, 6–7 minutes. Add the star anise and orange zest, reduce the heat to low, and simmer, uncovered, until the flavors have blended, about 1 hour.

❁ Meanwhile, peel the mandarins by hand, being careful to remove as much of the white membrane and pith as possible. Using a very sharp knife, cut them crosswise into slices ¼ inch (6 mm) thick and place in a heatproof bowl.

❁ Pour the hot syrup over the satsuma slices. Let stand at room temperature for 1 hour before serving to let the flavors develop.

❁ To serve, spoon the satsuma slices into individual bowls along with some syrup and a star anise.

NUTRITIONAL ANALYSIS PER SERVING: Calories 262 (Kilojoules 1,100); Protein 1 g; Carbohydrates 67 g; Total Fat 0 g; Saturated Fat 0 g; Cholesterol 0 mg; Sodium 2 mg; Dietary Fiber 2 g

Peach Upside-Down Cake

PREP TIME: 20 MINUTES

COOKING TIME: 30 MINUTES

INGREDIENTS

⅓ cup (3 oz/90 g) unsalted butter, plus 1 tablespoon melted and cooled

¾ cup (6 oz/185 g) firmly packed brown sugar

5 large, ripe O'Henry peaches, peeled, halved, and pitted

2 teaspoons crème de pêche (optional)

4 eggs

1 teaspoon almond extract (essence)

1 cup (4 oz/125 g) all-purpose (plain) flour

1 teaspoon baking powder

¼ teaspoon salt

1 cup (8 oz/250 g) granulated sugar

PREP TIP: To peel a peach or other stone fruit, immerse it in boiling water for about 10 seconds. Lift it out with a slotted spoon and transfer to a bowl filled with ice and water. Slip off the peel, using a small, sharp knife to assist you if necessary.

O'Henry peaches are exceptionally sweet and juicy when ripe, but any peach variety will work well in this recipe. Crème de pêche is a sweet French peach liqueur.

SERVES 6–8

❋ Preheat an oven to 350°F (180°C).

❋ In a 9- or 10-inch (23- or 25-cm) cast-iron or other ovenproof frying pan over medium heat, melt the ⅓ cup (3 oz/90 g) butter. Add the brown sugar and cook, stirring, until the sugar dissolves and forms a syrup, 6–7 minutes. Remove from the heat.

❋ Snugly pack the peach halves, cut sides up, onto the butter-sugar mixture and sprinkle with the crème de pêche, if using. Set aside.

❋ Separate the eggs, dropping the whites into a large bowl and the yolks into a medium one. Whisk the 1 tablespoon melted butter and the almond extract into the egg yolks and set aside.

❋ In another bowl, sift together the flour, baking powder, and salt.

❋ Using an electric mixer set on medium speed or a whisk, beat the egg whites just until they form firm peaks; do not overbeat. Using a rubber spatula, fold the granulated sugar, about ¼ cup (2 oz/60 g) at a time, into the egg whites. Then fold in the egg yolk mixture, about one-fourth at a time. Finally, fold in the flour mixture, about ¼ cup (1¼ oz/37 g) at a time. Pour the batter over the peaches and spread with the spatula to cover evenly.

❋ Bake until a toothpick inserted into the center comes out clean, about 30 minutes. Remove from the oven and let stand for 10 minutes. The cake will pull away slightly from the pan sides. To unmold, run a knife or an icing spatula around the inside edge of the pan to loosen the cake sides. Invert a large plate or platter on top of the frying pan and, holding the plate and frying pan tightly together with pot holders, flip them. Lift off the frying pan. Carefully replace any peach halves that are dislodged.

❋ Serve warm or at room temperature.

NUTRITIONAL ANALYSIS PER SERVING: Calories 479 (Kilojoules 2,012); Protein 6 g; Carbohydrates 86 g; Total Fat 14 g; Saturated Fat 7 g; Cholesterol 149 mg; Sodium 199 mg; Dietary Fiber 3 g

Chocolate Meringues with Summer Berry Sauce

PREP TIME: 20 MINUTES

COOKING TIME: 1 HOUR, PLUS
2 HOURS FOR COOLING

INGREDIENTS

6 egg whites, at room temperature

1½ teaspoons cream of tartar

½ teaspoon salt

1 teaspoon vanilla extract (essence)

2⅔ cups (21 oz/655 g) sugar

⅔ cup (2 oz/60 g) Dutch-process
cocoa powder

2 cups (8 oz/250 g) blackberries

2 cups (8 oz/250 g) boysenberries

3 cups (12 oz/375 g) raspberries

¼ cup (2 fl oz/60 ml) water

PREP TIP: If the air is humid, the meringues will absorb some of the moisture. Although this doesn't affect the flavor of the meringues, you may end up with ones that are slightly chewy on the outside rather than crisp.

Make this lusciously rich dessert when summer berries are abundant at farmers' markets. The meringues are cookie shaped, crisp on the outside, and chewy on the inside.

MAKES ABOUT 15 MERINGUES

❀ Preheat an oven to 250°F (120°C). Line a baking sheet with parchment (baking) paper.

❀ In a bowl, combine the egg whites, cream of tartar, and salt. Using an electric mixer set on medium speed, beat until soft peaks form. Add the vanilla and beat in briefly. Then beat in 1½ cups (12 oz/375 g) of the sugar alternately with the cocoa, about 2 tablespoons at a time in each case, beating well after each addition. Continue beating until the egg whites are stiff and glossy.

❀ To form each meringue, using a large spoon, scoop up about ¾ cup (6 fl oz/180 ml) of the egg-white mixture and drop it onto the paper to make a mound 2–2½ inches (5–6 cm) in diameter. Space the meringues about 1½ inches (4 cm) apart, as they will spread when they are baked. You should have about 15 mounds.

❀ Bake until firm, about 1 hour. Turn off the oven and let the meringues stand in the oven until completely cool, at least 2 hours or preferably as long as overnight. (If not using immediately, store in an airtight container in a dry place for up to 1 week.)

❀ In a bowl, combine the blackberries and boysenberries. Sprinkle ½ cup (4 oz/125 g) sugar over them, and toss gently to coat evenly. Set aside.

❀ In a saucepan over medium-high heat, combine the raspberries, the remaining ⅔ cup (5 oz/155 g) sugar, and the water. Bring to a boil, stirring constantly with a wooden spoon. Cook, stirring and mashing the berries with the back of the spoon, until the sugar dissolves, most of the raspberries are crushed, and a thickened sauce has formed, about 10 minutes. Remove from the heat. Pass the sauce through a food mill fitted with the fine shredding disk or a fine sieve placed over a bowl. Let cool.

❀ To serve, spoon about 1 teaspoon of the raspberry sauce onto a plate. Lay 2 meringues on top and scatter with a few berries.

NUTRITIONAL ANALYSIS PER MERINGUE: Calories 198 (Kilojoules 832); Protein 3 g; Carbohydrates 48 g; Total Fat 1 g; Saturated Fat 0 g; Cholesterol 0 mg; Sodium 127 mg; Dietary Fiber 2 g

Chocolate-Dipped Whole Dried Apricots with Almond Filling

PREP TIME: 30 MINUTES, PLUS
30 MINUTES FOR DRYING

COOKING TIME: 5 MINUTES

INGREDIENTS

½ cup (2 oz/60 g) almonds

3 oz (90 g) almond paste

24 dried whole apricots

2 oz (60 g) semisweet (plain)
   chocolate

One of the pleasures of wintertime farmers' markets is the opportunity to purchase farmer-dried fruits and nuts, which make a classic combination for eating out of hand. In this fancy variation, the fruits are stuffed with a nut mixture and then dipped in chocolate. Be sure to use almond paste, not marzipan, in this recipe; the former is more coarsely textured and less sweet than the latter. Dried whole apricots are also called "slip pits," as the pits are slipped from the fruits before drying.

MAKES 24

❀ In a blender or food processor, process the almonds to a fine meal. Transfer to a bowl and add the almond paste. Using a wooden spoon, stir to form a mixture with the texture of a soft dough. Using the end of the wooden spoon, stuff about ½ teaspoon of the almond mixture into the open end of each apricot.

❀ Put the chocolate in the top pan of a double boiler or in a heatproof bowl. Place over (not touching) gently boiling water in the bottom pan. Stir until melted and smooth, about 5 minutes. Remove the pan or bowl from over the water.

❀ Line a tray with waxed paper. Dip the open end of a filled apricot into the chocolate, allowing the chocolate to cover about one-third of the fruit. Set aside on the waxed paper–lined tray. Repeat with the remaining filled apricots. Let stand until dry and set, about 30 minutes.

❀ To store, place between layers of waxed paper in an airtight container. Store in a cool, dry place for up to 3 weeks.

NUTRITIONAL ANALYSIS PER APRICOT: Calories 58 (Kilojoules 244); Protein 1 g; Carbohydrates 8 g; Total Fat 3 g; Saturated Fat 1 g; Cholesterol 0 mg; Sodium 2 mg; Dietary Fiber 1 g

Spiced Wine Gelatin with Summer Fruits

PREP TIME: 40 MINUTES, PLUS 5 HOURS FOR CHILLING

COOKING TIME: 5 MINUTES

INGREDIENTS

¾ cup (6 fl oz/180 ml) Merlot, Pinot Noir, or Zinfandel wine

¾ cup (6 fl oz/180 ml) red wine vinegar

2½ cups (1¼ lb/625 g) sugar

1 cinnamon stick

1 fresh rosemary sprig

1 cup (8 fl oz/250 ml) cold water

2¼ tablespoons unflavored gelatin

1½ cups (12 fl oz/375 ml) boiling water

1 Elephant Heart or other large plum, cut lengthwise into slices ¼ inch (6 mm) thick

24 Flame or other seedless grapes, some left whole, others halved or quartered lengthwise

2 Adriatic or other figs, cut lengthwise into slices ¼ inch (6 mm) thick

1 yellow-fleshed nectarine, halved, pitted, and cut lengthwise into slices ¼ inch (6 mm) thick

In this refreshing and sparkling dessert, pieces of fruit are set in gelatin. The fruits suggested here make a particularly colorful dish, although others may be used. The gelatin can be made in one big mold or in individual glass custard cups.

SERVES 8

❁ In a nonaluminum saucepan over high heat, combine the wine, vinegar, sugar, cinnamon, and rosemary. Bring to a boil, stirring often. Boil, stirring constantly, until the sugar dissolves and a thin syrup forms, about 5 minutes. Remove from the heat and remove the cinnamon stick and rosemary sprig and discard.

❁ Pour the cold water into a heatproof bowl and sprinkle the gelatin over the surface. Let stand for 1 minute to soften. Return the wine mixture to a boil, then pour it into the bowl with the gelatin. Add the boiling water and stir until the gelatin is completely dissolved, 4–5 minutes. Pour into a 4-cup (32–fl oz/1-l) rectangular mold, such as a loaf pan, or divide it evenly among 8 glass custard cups. Drop the fruits into the gelatin, distributing them evenly. Let cool, then cover and refrigerate until the gelatin is set, at least 5 hours.

❁ To serve, scoop the gelatin from the mold into glass bowls or stemware, or present it in the custard cups.

NUTRITIONAL ANALYSIS PER SERVING: Calories 342 (Kilojoules 1,436); Protein 2 g; Carbohydrates 82 g; Total Fat 0 g; Saturated Fat 0 g; Cholesterol 0 mg; Sodium 6 mg; Dietary Fiber 1 g

Nectarine and Fig Cobbler

PREP TIME: 15 MINUTES

COOKING TIME: 35 MINUTES

INGREDIENTS

4 ripe, juicy white-fleshed nectarines, halved, pitted, and sliced (about 2 cups/12 oz/375 g)

1 lb (500 g) soft, ripe Mission or Adriatic figs, halved lengthwise

½ cup (4 oz/125 g) sugar

2 tablespoons plus 1 cup (5 oz/155 g) all-purpose (plain) flour

2 tablespoons water

1 teaspoon lemon juice

1¼ teaspoons baking powder

½ teaspoon salt

¼ cup (2 oz/60 g) chilled unsalted butter, cut into small pieces

¼ cup (2 fl oz/60 ml) milk

The distinct flavors of nectarines and figs are highlighted by a sweet, biscuitlike crust. For a juicy cobbler, use the ripest fruits you can find. For an extra treat, top each serving of warm cobbler with a scoop of vanilla ice cream.

SERVES 6

❀ Preheat an oven to 450°F (230°C).

❀ In a bowl, combine the nectarines and figs. In another bowl, stir together the sugar and the 2 tablespoons flour. Sprinkle the sugar-flour mixture over the fruit. Add the water and lemon juice and toss to coat evenly. Transfer to an 8-inch (20-cm) square baking dish with 2-inch (5-cm) sides.

❀ To make the crust, in a bowl, stir together the 1 cup (5 oz/155 g) flour, the baking powder, and salt. Using a pastry blender or 2 knives, cut the butter into the flour until the mixture forms pea-sized pieces. Gradually add the milk, tossing and stirring constantly with a wooden spoon, until the dough comes together. Using your hands, gather the dough into a ball. Place the ball on a floured work surface and, using your fingers, pat it out into a square about the same size as the baking dish and about ¼ inch (6 mm) thick.

❀ Carefully transfer the pastry to the top of the baking dish. Trim away any excess dough.

❀ Bake for 20 minutes. Reduce the heat to 300°F (150°C) and continue to bake until the crust is a deep golden brown, 10–15 minutes longer. Transfer to a rack to cool. Scoop out the cobbler onto dessert plates and serve warm.

NUTRITIONAL ANALYSIS PER SERVING: Calories 327 (Kilojoules 1,373); Protein 4 g; Carbohydrates 61 g; Total Fat 9 g; Saturated Fat 5 g; Cholesterol 22 mg; Sodium 302 mg; Dietary Fiber 4 g

Pomelo-Mint Sorbet

PREP TIME: 20 MINUTES

COOKING TIME: 5 MINUTES,
   PLUS 6 HOURS FOR
   CHILLING

INGREDIENTS

1 cup (8 oz/250 g) sugar

1 cup (1 oz/30 g) fresh mint leaves,
   plus sprigs for garnish

1 cup (8 fl oz/250 ml) water

2 cups (16 fl oz/500 ml) strained
   pomelo juice (from about 3
   pomelos)

1 tablespoon lemon juice

3 tablespoons minced pomelo zest,
   plus strips for garnish (optional)

Pomelos, which look and taste much like grapefruits except that they are larger and somewhat less juicy, make an excellent sweet-tart sorbet. If pomelos are unavailable, use grapefruits instead. Fresh mint flavors the syrup before it is frozen and garnishes the sorbet when it's ready to serve.

MAKES ABOUT 1½ PINTS (24 FL OZ/750 ML); SERVES 6

❈ In a small saucepan over medium heat, combine the sugar, mint leaves, and water. Bring to a boil over high heat, stirring to dissolve the sugar. Reduce the heat to medium-low and simmer uncovered, stirring constantly, until a thin syrup forms, about 5 minutes. Remove from the heat and let stand for 10 minutes. Add the pomelo and lemon juices, then cover and refrigerate for at least 6 hours or for up to overnight.

❈ Strain through a fine-mesh sieve to remove the mint leaves, then stir in the minced zest. Freeze in an ice-cream maker according to the manufacturer's directions.

❈ To serve, spoon into individual bowls and garnish with mint sprigs and zest strips, if you like.

NUTRITIONAL ANALYSIS PER SERVING: Calories 182 (Kilojoules 764); Protein 1 g; Carbohydrates 46 g; Total Fat 0 g; Saturated Fat 0 g; Cholesterol 0 mg; Sodium 3 mg; Dietary Fiber 0 g

Quince Poached in Lemon-Vanilla Syrup

PREP TIME: 15 MINUTES

COOKING TIME: 30 MINUTES,
    PLUS 15 MINUTES FOR
    COOLING

INGREDIENTS

2½ cups (1¼ lb/625 g) sugar

2 cups (16 fl oz/500 ml) water

1 vanilla bean

2 tablespoons lemon juice

3 quinces, peeled, halved, cored,
    and sliced lengthwise ½ inch
    (12 mm) thick

1½ teaspoons grated lemon zest,
    plus strips for garnish

Quince is an old-fashioned fruit, inedible when raw because of its intense astringency. Its flesh is white but turns a lovely amber and sweetens when cooked. The quince is a pome fruit like the apple and pear and, once cooked, resembles them somewhat in texture.

SERVES 4

❀ In a saucepan large enough to hold the quinces, combine the sugar, water, vanilla bean, and lemon juice. Bring to a boil over medium-high heat, stirring to dissolve the sugar. Then boil, stirring often, until a light-to-medium-thick syrup forms, about 10 minutes.

❀ Add the quinces and reduce the heat to low. Add the grated lemon zest and poach the fruit, uncovered, until tender when pierced with a fork, about 20 minutes. Remove from the heat and let stand until the syrup is nearly at room temperature, about 15 minutes.

❀ To serve, ladle several pieces of fruit into individual bowls or glasses with some of the syrup. Garnish with the strips of lemon zest.

NUTRITIONAL ANALYSIS PER SERVING: Calories 319 (Kilojoules 1,340); Protein 0 g; Carbohydrates 83 g; Total Fat 0 g; Saturated Fat 0 g; Cholesterol 0 mg; Sodium 4 mg; Dietary Fiber 0 g

GLOSSARY

ASPARAGUS

Tender asparagus shoots start pushing up through the earth in early spring and reach their peak of flavor late in the season. Look in farmers' markets for the usual green asparagus, as well as for purple-tinged varieties and ivory-colored spears, the latter produced by covering the shoots with earth to blanch them as they grow. Choose asparagus with tightly closed buds and with stem ends that look freshly cut.

BROCCOLI RABE

Also known as rapini, rape, or raab, this pleasantly bitter, strong-flavored green is actually a closer botanical relative to turnips than to the broccoli it resembles. Its slender stalks, small florets, and deep green leaves have a strong, bitter, slightly nutlike flavor that goes well with pungent seasonings such as garlic and anchovies. You'll find it in farmers' markets from autumn into spring.

CABBAGE, NAPA

Available year-round but at its peak in colder months, this cabbage variety is enjoyed raw or cooked for its crisp leaves, which are distinctively crinkled, long, and pale green to white. Also called celery cabbage or Chinese cabbage.

CHEESES

Many different cheeses complement the vegetables and fruits available at farmers' markets. Those used in this book include **fresh goat cheese,** sold at some farmer' markets and enjoyed for its creamy texture and its rich, tangy flavor; **Monterey jack,** a soft, mild, slightly tangy cow's milk cheese traditionally produced in California; **Parmesan,** the hard, firm-textured, well-aged cow's milk cheese of Italy, of which the finest variety, designated Parmigiano-Reggiano®, is made only from midspring to midautumn, then aged for at least 14 months; and California **teleme,** a rich, creamy cow's milk cheese resembling Brie.

CHILES

Many good-sized farmers' markets carry chiles, particularly in summer when fresh ones are most abundant. There are scores of varieties of fresh and dried chiles, in a wide range of shapes, sizes, and colors. Some chiles are sweet, others astringent, and although they have a reputation for being hot, some are surprisingly mild. Cut out the ribs and discard the seeds and a hot chile will become less so. The varieties called for in this book include the **Anaheim** (below), also

known as long green or California chile, a large, slender green specimen that can be mild or slightly hot; the **jalapeño** (below, top),

a familiar fresh green (or less often ripened red) chile that ranges from mild to scorching hot; the **pasilla,** a dried chile enjoyed for its rich, moderately hot, slightly sweet flavor; and the slender **serrano** (above, bottom), a green or red "mountain" chile about 2 inches (5 cm) long, with a taste as hot as, but distinctly sharper than, the jalapeño.

FENNEL

Related to the fresh herb of the same name, this cool weather vegetable resembles a rounded head of celery. Eaten raw in salads or cooked alone or with other ingredients, it is enjoyed for its crisp texture and mild, sweet anise flavor. The stalks may also be used, added as a seasoning to simmered dishes or roasts, and the feathery tops make an attractive and tasty garnish.

GARLIC

This pungent seasoning, a member of the onion family, is found mature and freshly harvested in farmers' markets during summer. For the best flavor, buy no more than you will use in 1–2 weeks and store in a cool, dry place. During springtime, watch market stalls for the appearance of **green garlic** (right), immature heads that have been harvested before their individual cloves form and are enjoyed for their sweet and mild flavor.

GINGER

Although fresh ginger resembles a root, this sweet-hot seasoning is actually the underground stem, or rhizome, of the tropical ginger plant. Knobby pieces of fresh ginger may be found year-round in farmers' market stalls, with the youngest, freshest ginger harvested in springtime and recognized by its edible, creamy skin and pink tips.

HERBS

Fresh herbs are widely available year-round, although farmers' markets are likely to sell many herbs only in spring and summer, when they are at their most abundant and least expensive. The herbs used in this book include:

BASIL

This spicy-sweet, tender-leaved herb goes especially well in dishes featuring tomatoes, as well as other vegetables, rice, seafood, and chicken. Beside common green basil, look for **dark opal** or **purple basil**, which has a spicier taste reminiscent of ginger, and milder, sweeter-tasting Thai basil, at its peak in springtime.

BAY LEAVES

The whole leaves of the bay laurel tree have a pungent, spicy flavor. Seek out the French variety, which has a milder, sweeter flavor than California bay leaves. Unlike dried bay leaves, which store well and are added to dishes whole, fresh leaves should be used within a few days of purchase and may be torn into smaller pieces before they are added to a dish.

CHERVIL

A springtime herb, chervil has a taste reminiscent of parsley and anise. It goes particularly well with poultry and seafood, with carrots, and in salads.

CHIVES

These slender, bright green stems of a plant related to the onion deliver an onionlike flavor without the bite. They are at their best when fresh and raw, as drying or cooking diminishes their character. In springtime, look for chives sold with their pretty, delicately flavored purple blossoms still attached. Chives complement egg dishes, vegetables, and salads.

CILANTRO

Also known as fresh coriander and Chinese parsley, cilantro has flat, frilly leaves that resemble those of flat-leaf (Italian) parsley. Its flavor is slightly grassy and a little astringent. Cilantro is popular in Latin American, Middle Eastern, and Asian dishes.

DILL

The sprightly taste of this feathery-leaved herb, which goes well with seafood, chicken, mild cheeses, and vegetables, is lost when it is not at its freshest or when it is cooked. To guarantee the best flavor, buy dill with bright green leaves and stems. Look for tiny, delicate baby dill if possible, and add it to dishes just before serving.

MARJORAM

This Mediterranean herb, which has a milder flavor than its close relative, oregano, is best used fresh. Pair it with tomatoes, eggplant, beans, poultry, and seafood.

MINT

A popular seasoning for springtime lamb, poultry, vegetables, fruits, and various desserts, this refreshingly sweet herb grows wild in many parts of the world. Of the many different species cultivated, spearmint is the most commonly sold.

PARSLEY

The **flat-leaf (Italian)** variety of this well-known fresh herb is more pronounced in flavor than the common curly type, making it preferable as a seasoning. It goes well with all manner of savory dishes.

ROSEMARY

Used fresh or dried, this Mediterranean herb has a strong, fragrant flavor well suited to meats, poultry, seafood, and vegetables. It is particularly favored as a seasoning for chicken or lamb, and also complements pork or veal.

SAGE

Soft, gray-green sage leaves are sweet and aromatic. Used fresh or dried, they pair well with poultry, vegetables, and fresh or cured pork.

TARRAGON

With its distinctively sweet flavor reminiscent of anise, tarragon is used to season many salads and egg and vegetable dishes, as well as mild-tasting main-course ingredients such as chicken and fish.

THYME

One of the most important culinary herbs of Europe, thyme delivers a floral, earthy flavor to all types of food, including vegetables, especially roots and tubers, and nearly every kind of poultry.

WINTER SAVORY

This shrublike Mediterranean evergreen herb, often grown alongside milder-tasting summer savory to provide year-round availability, has a strong, spicy flavor that some cooks liken to thyme. It goes well with dried beans and lentils, meats, poultry, tomatoes, and other vegetables.

HORSERADISH, FRESH

A distant cousin of mustard, this root vegetable is powerfully pungent when grated, releasing intensely flavorful oils. Look for it year-round in farmers' markets.

JERUSALEM ARTICHOKES

These tuberous vegetables, which resemble small potatoes, get their name in part because their flavor resembles an artichoke and in part because of their botanical kinship to the sunflower, *girasole* in Italian. They are at their best and most abundant in farmers' markets during winter.

KALE

At its peak of season from late autumn through winter, this leafy green member of the mustard family is prized for the strong, spicy taste and robust texture of its leaves, best enjoyed cooked. Farmers' markets may offer a variety of types, with leaves of different shapes and in colors ranging from blue-green to red, purple to yellow or white. Be sure to remove the leaves from their tough stems before cooking.

LEEKS

At their best from early spring through autumn, leeks are sweet and mild when cooked. **Baby leeks**, harvested in spring and found in some farmers' markets, have a particularly delicate taste and texture. The tender white parts of fully grown leeks have the mildest flavor and are often used alone; the tougher greens, however, may be included in long-cooked dishes. Grown in sandy soil, leeks should be rinsed thoroughly with cold running water to remove any grit lodged between their leaves. Slit them lengthwise to make cleaning easier.

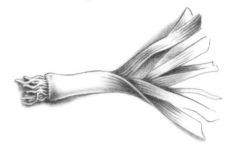

LEMONS, MEYER

Sold in farmers' markets from spring into early summer, these round, juicy citrus fruits have a much sweeter flavor and more intense aroma than more common lemons, as well as a thinner, softer, milder-tasting peel.

OILS

Nearly tasteless oils such as **corn oil, canola oil,** or other light **vegetable oils** are excellent for all-purpose cooking. So, too, is **pure olive oil,** which has been blended and refined. **Extra-virgin olive oils,** by contrast, are generally fruity and full flavored; use them for dressing salads or as a condiment. **Asian sesame oil,** pressed from roasted sesame seeds, is used as a seasoning or condiment. Do not confuse it with the lighter-hued, less-flavorful cold-pressed sesame oil sold in health-food stores and well-stocked food stores. Store all oils in airtight containers at cool room temperature, away from light.

ONIONS

From spring into summer, farmers' markets offer a good selection of just-harvested onions. Those called for in this book include **green (spring) onions,** also known as scallions, which are long, slender white bulbs harvested and sold immature, leaves and all; sweet, purple-and-white **red (Spanish) onions,** including the very sweet **torpedo** variety (above, right) named for its elongated shape; and **yellow onions,** the most commonly available, distinguished by their dry, yellowish brown skins and strong-flavored white flesh.

PANCETTA

A specialty of the Emilia-Romagna region of northern Italy, this unsmoked bacon is cured with salt and pepper. It is sold either in slabs like bacon or rolled and is used to add a rich undertone of flavor to long-simmered dishes or stuffings. Look for pancetta in well-stocked food stores and Italian delicatessens.

PARSNIPS

With a shape, size, and texture similar to carrots, these root vegetables are available from autumn through spring. They are at their best, however, after prolonged exposure to winter's cold—whether while still in the earth or in cold storage—has converted their starch to sugar.

PEPPERS

Farmers' markets, particularly in summer, offer a wide variety of sweet peppers (capsicums). As **bell peppers,** descriptively named for their shape, ripen, they change from green to red or to other colors such as orange or yellow. Also, look for somewhat sweeter **Italian peppers** and for deep red, spicy-sweet **pimientos,** both of which resemble elongated bell peppers. Pimientos are most commonly available in jars in food stores.

PERSIMMONS

Found in farmers' markets from autumn into winter, these vividly orange native Asian fruits have shiny, smooth skins and delectably tart-sweet flesh. Two basic types are grown and sold. The **Hachiya persimmon** (below), recognizable by its heart shape, requires ripening until it is mushy soft, at which point its sharply astringent flavor disappears.

The rounder **Fuyu persimmon** (below) has none of that astringency and will remain quite firm and crisp when ripe.

POTATOES

In spring and summer, some of the finest potatoes fill the stalls of farmers' markets. Earlier in the year, look for **new potatoes**, small, immature specimens that are harvested while their skins are papery and their waxy flesh is delicate and sweet. Summer is the time for such distinctive types as the **fingerling potato** (below), a waxy variety notable for

its long, very slender shape; the **Red Rose**, a common variety of small, round, red-skinned, waxy-fleshed potato; and **Yellow Finn** and **Yukon gold potatoes**, both prized for the deep yellow of their waxy flesh, which has a rich, almost buttery flavor.

PURSLANE

Occasionally found in farmers' markets during its summer season, purslane is distinguished by its small, rounded leaves that grow on the ends of green or red stems. The leaves have a crisp, juicy texture and a mild, sweet taste that make them a good addition to salads and some cooked dishes.

QUINCES

Resembling oversized, ungainly apples or pears, these winter fruits are only enjoyed cooked; raw quinces have a rough texture and harsh taste. Their high pectin content makes them ideal for jams or jellies. Before cooking, skin and core quinces, rubbing their exposed flesh with lemon juice to prevent discoloration as you would for an apple or pear.

RADICCHIO

Available from autumn through spring, this member of the chicory family is noted for its compact heads of usually purple-red leaves, which have a crisp texture and a refreshing edge of bitterness. Among the many varieties you might find in a farmers' market, look for **Treviso**, with its long, pointed, red-fringed leaves and white ribs. Radicchio may be eaten either raw in salads or cooked, often by grilling.

SALT, ROCK

Coarse-grained rock salt is available in well-stocked food stores. It's not refined as much as table salt and is predominantly used as a bed for ingredients in salt-roasting and ice cream making.

SHALLOTS

These members of the onion family have paper-thin, copper-colored skins covering pale, purple-tinged flesh. They have a crisp texture and a more refined, milder flavor than the onion.

SQUASH FLOWERS

In summer and autumn, the flowers of zucchini (courgettes) and other squashes may sometimes be found in farmers' markets, sold either separately or still attached to the squash. Prized for their highly delicate flavor and texture, they are best cooked on the day of purchase.

VINEGARS

The word vinegar literally means "sour wine," describing what results when certain strains of yeast cause wine to ferment for a second time, turning it sharply acidic. The best-quality wine vinegars begin with good-quality wine. **Red wine vinegar**, like the wine from which it is made, has a more robust flavor than vinegar produced from white wine. Italian **balsamic vinegar**, a highly prized specialty of Modena, starts with cooked and reduced grape juice, which is aged for many years in a progression of ever-smaller barrels made of different woods, to produce a vinegar of almost syruplike consistency, with a complex and intense flavor. **Rice vinegar**, by contrast, has a light, clean flavor reflecting the Asian rice wine from which it is made.

INDEX

ACKNOWLEDGMENTS

The publishers would like to thank the following people and associations for their generous support and assistance in producing this book:
Desne Border, Ken DellaPenta, and Hill Nutrition Associates.

The following kindly lent props for photography: The Gardener, Berkeley, CA; and Fillamento, Williams-Sonoma, and Pottery Barn, San Francisco, CA. The photographer would like to thank Helie Robertson for generously sharing her home for location photography. He would also like to thank Chromeworks and ProCamera, San Francisco, CA, and FUJI film for their generous support of this project. Special acknowledgment goes to Daniel Yearwood for the beautiful backgrounds and surface treatments.